SHIP

OF

FOOLS

OTHER BOOKS
BY C. R. HALLPIKE

Do We Need God to be Good?
An anthropologist considers the evidence

Ethical Thought in Increasingly Complex Societies:
Social structure and moral development

On Primitive Society, and other forbidden topics

How We Got Here. From bows and arrows to the space age

The Konso of Ethiopia:
A study of the Values of an East Cushitic Society

The Evolution of Moral Understanding

The Principles of Social Evolution

The Foundations of Primitive Thought

SHIP
OF
FOOLS

An anthology of learned nonsense about primitive society

C. R. HALLPIKE

CASTALIA HOUSE

Ship of Fools: An Anthology of Learned Nonsense About Primitive Society

C. R. Hallpike

Published by Castalia House
Kouvola, Finland
www.castaliahouse.com

Cover Painting: "Ship of Fools", by Hieronymous Bosch

ISBN: 978-952-7065-55-6

The crew are all quarrelling with each other about how to navigate the ship, each thinking he ought to be at the helm; they know no navigation and cannot say that anyone ever taught it them, or that they spent any time studying it; indeed they say it can't be taught and are ready to murder anyone who says it can. They spend all their time milling round the captain and trying to get him to give them the wheel.... They have no idea that the true navigator must study the seasons of the year, the sky, the stars, the winds and other professional subjects, if he is to be really fit to control a ship.

—Plato, *The Republic*, Bk. VI, Tr. H.D.P. Lee

Contents

Preface

I spent my first ten or so years as an anthropologist either living with mountain tribes in Ethiopia and Papua New Guinea or writing up my research for publication. These more primitive types of society are small-scale, face-to-face, without writing, money, or the state, organized on the basis of kinship, age, and gender, and with subsistence economies. As such they are very different from our own modern industrialised societies and it takes a good deal of study to understand how they work. But since all our ancestors used to live like this, understanding them is essential to understanding the human race itself, especially when speculating about our prehistoric ancestors in East Africa. Unfortunately a variety of journalists and science writers, historians, linguists, biologists, and especially evolutionary psychologists think they are qualified to write about primitive societies without knowing much about them, or, even worse, think that a political agenda justifies them in falsifying the record. The result in many cases has resembled a Ship of Fools, True Believers in some pet ideology like extreme neo-Darwinism, or social justice, or some will o' the wisp of their own imaginations, and many of their speculations have about as much scientific credibility as The Flintstones. So the various critical studies in this little book are offered as a sort of bouquet or anthology of nonsense about primitive man, and I only hope my readers derive as much entertainment from them as I have had in writing them.

C.R.H.
Shipton Moyne
Gloucestershire
August 2018

Talking nonsense about primitive society

1. What primitive societies are actually like

Before joining the Ship of Fools I thought it might be useful if I began with a rough guide to what primitive societies are like.

The most powerful impact of primitive society on the anthropologist is what I can only call the sheer immediacy and intimacy of the physical world when it is experienced with virtually no technology—only human muscles, only the spoken word, only face-to-face communication, and only a few simple tools. In our WEIRD culture (Western, Educated, Industrialised, Rich, Democratic)[1], we experience the physical world to a great extent through our technology. Instead of walking, for example, we encounter the countryside through our cars, we talk to family, friends and neighbours over the telephone, and when we want water we turn on a tap, which brings it from some fairly distant part of the country by a huge system of reservoirs, pumping stations and pipes. In primitive societies, however, someone, almost invariably a woman, has to go and fetch it themselves from a water-hole, or stream, or well, in a bamboo or gourd container, or perhaps in a clay pot and carry it wearily home, sometimes several times a day.

In the primitive world everything is made by the people themselves, not out of metals and plastic in remote factories in other countries but out of familiar local materials—wood, plants to use for thatching, thread or baskets, gourd or bamboo containers, stones for building and tools, and animal products like hide, sinew, and bone, while there may be little or no metal. The primitive world is also very small and human-sized. There are no great cities or gigantic multi-storey concrete buildings, just villages of small huts thatched with grass or palm leaves, the roof held up by wooden posts and maybe some wattle and daub to keep the draughts out, and with no furniture like tables, chairs and beds, let alone anything comfortable like sofas and armchairs. There is just the bare ground to sleep or to sit on, except perhaps for an animal skin, and with no tables to put anything on either. People grow the food they eat, probably very limited in variety, in the gardens and fields they own, and bring it home on, usually, the women's backs though in some societies there may be donkeys or other beasts of burden.

So life is extremely hard, and the food is usually dreadful. Members of our intelligentsia who chatter about the joys of this kind of life would probably have to be medically evacuated after a few weeks if they actually had to live with them under their traditional conditions of existence. The basic Konso meal, for example, mainly consisted of boiled sorghum dough and tree leaves, eaten three times a day, and sorghum is an unappetising cereal that is regarded by northern Ethiopians as fit only for cattle. *Chaqa*, the beer made from it, is a sour alcoholic grain soup, usually served hot, which compares unfavourably with Ethiopian *tej* (honey wine) or beer made from barley. While Konso coffee is excellent, traditionally it was not drunk but the beans were roasted and eaten on ritual occasions, and honey was not used to make a drink either. Milk, if available, is drunk only by children, and butter, which is very expensive, is used more as a cosmetic than as an item of diet. Meat, to be sure, is sold in the markets as a luxury, but there is a notable absence in Konso of the spices which elsewhere in Ethiopia are used to produce a range of appetising dishes. Chickens were kept in the traditional society, but only for their feathers, since it was forbidden to eat any kinds of bird or their eggs.

The Tauade of Papua New Guinea grew sweet-potatoes, which are a good deal tastier than sorghum, and much easier to prepare, as well as yams and taro, with pork and smoked pandanus nuts as treats. But since meat in farming societies is a luxury, people are none too fussy about its quality. Garide, my Konso cook, and I had been up to the market one day to buy some meat and had brought it back in a plastic bag. In the hot season in Africa this is not a good idea, and when we came to open it some hours later the stench was appalling. A man happened to be passing the doorway of my house, however, and was very keen to buy it for the small sum we were asking and snapped up his bargain with alacrity. In Papua New Guinea the people are even less fastidious about their pork when it is stinking, even cutting it up under water when the smell is too bad. And yes, sometimes they died from it. Biologists often tell us that we are protected by the vomiting reflex from eating meat that has begun to smell as it goes bad, but no one seems to have told primitive peoples about this.

While the Konso had cattle, as well as sheep and goats, they couldn't use them to plough, as their fields consisted of narrow stone-built terraces which made ploughing impossible. For tilling and weeding they had to use hoes, and everything they made or did was based on gruelling human labour under the African sun with nothing in the way of machines, except the loom for weaving. The Tauade were even simpler farmers with stone tools and no traditional knowledge of metal, and whose animals were simply pigs and dogs; they could only till the ground with wooden sticks, did not use manure like the Konso, and so had to make fresh gardens every three years or so by cutting down the bush with stone tools and burning it.

The anthropologist must simply get used to the public slaughter of animals. A few days after I arrived in Buso, for example, (the Konso village where I first lived) a goat was sacrificed outside my front door. At the moment of sacrifice the goat was held up in the air: "there, held up by his four legs, he stayed for about thirty seconds, and then had a spear pushed into his chest. He looked round in a bewildered way, and gave a dreadful cry, which was echoed joyfully by the men and boys. Some more spears were thrust into him and he gave some more horrible cries. They finished him off on the ground with knives, pretty crudely, with much gurgling and shrieking" (2008: 364-5). The killing of pigs among the Tauade was also a formal occasion, though not a sacrifice, because there was a taboo against killing one's own pigs: "They are like our own children", I was told, so someone else had to do it for them. This led to ceremonial killings at which speeches were made, followed by the killing of the pigs which was done by beating them over the head with the equivalent of baseball bats as they lay on the ground. The thuds of the blows, the shrieks of the dying animals, and the blood streaming from their nostrils being lapped up by the village dogs took some getting used to. At my first pig-killing somebody varied the procedure by shooting one of the pigs with a 12-bore shotgun in the face, while another large boar was put on the fire (to singe off the bristles) while still alive and screaming horribly. (They did, however, agree to my request to club it more thoroughly and put it out of its misery.)

Inside the Konso sleeping huts there were giant cockroaches, scorpions, poisonous centipedes, rats, and the occasional cobra. People generally slept on the ground on cow-skins, and the only wooden bedstead I encountered was infested with bed-bugs. To go to the lavatory they went to screened-off places on the edge of the towns, and when the faeces had dried they were mixed with animal manure to be spread on the terraces. Not surprisingly human manure also attracted the flies, which then settled on the childrens' eyes and gave them severe conjunctivitis. The mothers would bring them to me with their eyelids gummed together with pus, and when I had finally washed them sufficiently to get the eyes open they would usually run with blood, so severe was the infection. The children were also particularly troubled with head-lice and often had their heads shaved as a result. There is little in the way of medicines, and while the Konso had some traditional remedies for minor ailments, they were essentially defenceless against serious illness and had to trust to their natural resilience. The Tauade were in a similar situation, but living in much smaller settlements at a higher altitude and with more rainfall they were less subject to diseases.

Again, we take light so much for granted now, in our electric civilisation, but going to live in a primitive society it is a real shock, after the very brief tropical twilight, to encounter the profound darkness that can fall after the sun has gone down, especially when there is no moon. Without candles or lamps, people only had light from fires, or perhaps a burning brand in emergencies. I well remember how demoralising it was when my pressure lantern would suddenly go out and the brilliant, comforting light all around me would vanish and leave me with the dim glow of my hurricane lamp, and there was no way of investigating those disturbing sounds—is that a snake, or just rats? Konso homesteads had lots of stone walls, and one could put one's hand in the dark on a cobra looking for rats. The night was filled with threatening supernatural presences as well, and my cook, Garide, told me that he hated walking home to his village every night when he left me because the path took him through a sacred grove where he could hear the ghosts talking. Ghosts, evil spirits, magic and witchcraft are universal aspects of primitive life, and recognition of this is one of the most important intellectual adjustments that modern Westerners have to make when living in these societies.

Where water is scarce and is arduous to fetch, drinking and cooking take priority over hygiene by a wide margin, and I never saw the Konso (or the Tauade, for that matter) wash their hands before eating. The Konso women liked to put butter in their hair to make it shine, and especially at dances it would run down their chests in black rivulets. They wore leather caps on their buttered hair, and their skirts were also of leather, which was very hard-wearing but could not be cleaned, and in any case they had no soap or detergents to do so, even for their cotton blankets and the men's shorts.

Most primitive peoples live in the tropics, which means that they don't actually *need* to wear any clothes at all, but for reasons of sexual modesty most wear some sort of genital covering, particularly women. This is quite easy to make out of leaves or something similar, but garments for the rest of the body are quite another thing. Konso women wore rather elaborate leather skirts, even as little girls in their mother's arms, because they had a strong taboo against exposing the female genitals, but bare breasts were a different matter and before the arrival of European clothes Konso women were all bare-breasted, like those of a vast number of other cultures. They were more relaxed about male nudity, and while men in my time wore simple shorts, it was said that in the past they had worked naked in the fields. Large garments to cover the body, however, rather than just the genital area, are extremely difficult to produce unless they are made from skins. The Konso men in particular wore large cotton blankets, like a toga, and these required professional weavers with looms, and many people to spin the large amounts of thread required. But larger garments of this size are generally worn for purely social reasons, such as to convey dignity of appearance, rank, occupation, and so forth. So it is only in modern times when European-style garments have become available that they have been taken up in primitive society. The Tauade apparently adopted European dress not because either the Catholic Mission or the government encouraged them to do so but because they hoped that by looking like the white man they would also somehow become rich. Since the end of the nineteenth century the Konso have been governed by the Amhara, who are a literate and sophisticated people, and who very much disapprove of the bare breasts of Konso women. It seems that this pressure, together with a fashionable appetite for modern dress, have been the major factors behind the adoption of clothes by the Konso.

In primitive societies unmarried adults, unless their spouse has died, are very uncommon, because marriage is an economic and social necessity. Some people may have a romantic image of primitive society as beautiful scantily-dressed girls with flowers in their hair making love with all and sundry. There was some truth in this as the early navigators discovered in Polynesia, where there was plenty of water for bathing, and a luxuriant and undemanding climate. Away from the beaches, however, the vast majority of primitive societies are very far from being erotic paradises, which need cleanliness and leisure. Water may be too scarce for much in the way of washing, so that people are pretty dusty, dirty, and sweaty, and what clothes they have will be fairly stinky, and the women especially have to work very hard. While some societies like the Tauade were sexually promiscuous, others like the Konso were not, and adultery was severely punished. In primitive society there is generally no accepted idea of romantic love in the culture, though no doubt some people may feel it. Evolutionary biologists have an individualistic image of "mates" freely choosing one another simply on the basis of some estimate of each other's fecundity, but this is quite unrealistic. Marriage in primitive society is very much not a matter of romantic love, or even of individual choice, and women in particular generally have to marry in accordance with custom and the wishes of their kin. I never saw married couples of the opposite sex kissing each other, or displaying other signs of physical affection either among the Konso or the Tauade, and I can only recall once seeing a Konso boy with his arm round a girl's neck.

The lack of clothing not only makes the naked body much more obvious than it is in our society, but where we might use clothes to make social statements, in primitive societies people tend to do things to their bodies instead, like putting bones through their noses or long gourds over their penises, wearing paints, scarifying their faces or bodies, cutting off finger joints in mourning, or wearing things such as bells on the ankles of unmarried girls, or a special shell on the forehead by a man to indicate he has killed someone. Taking body trophies of enemies killed in warfare like heads or genitals is also common, and the eating of enemies killed in battle used to occur in many societies.

Birth, sickness and death are also commonplaces of the body in daily life that everyone has to deal with, not hidden neatly away in professional establishments like hospitals, doctors' surgeries, or funeral parlours. It used to be Tauade practice in Papua New Guinea to keep the bodies of Big Men in elevated baskets, *tseetsi*, to rot. These were inside the hamlets, and according to my informants the stench was appalling, with maggots from the corpse crawling over people as they slept. When the corpse had rotted the bones were collected and washed, then put in string bags. These were brought out at major dances and given to the guests to dance with as a form of honouring the dead. It was also Tauade custom for women to cut off one of their finger-joints in mourning for husband or child, and I saw a number of old women missing the ends of their fingers; in earlier years they also used to wear body parts of the deceased. "A recently bereaved widow had an arm bone, several rib bones and the complete hand of the late departed hanging on a string around her neck. She did not appear to mind the offensive odour", as a patrol officer wrote in 1945. When I finally left, Amo Lume, my main informant, gave me his grandfather's skull, and a thighbone as leaving presents, and they are still on my desk. As one might expect, the Tauade were totally at ease with the remnants of the dead, and I remember Amo one day finding a bit of pelvis in my garden: "Oh, that'll be old So-and-so", he remarked, tossing it over his shoulder. The Konso of Ethiopia, however, were the exact opposite, and had a complete horror of death. As soon as someone died the body had to be carried out to the family fields wrapped in a cowskin, while the men of the ward got together to dig the grave so that the deceased was safely underground before the end of the day. They were particularly careful to beat the earth down hard to prevent the smell escaping and attracting hyenas.

The Tauade were happy to admit that they had been cannibals before the Australian administration had come, but they apparently did not go in for it in any elaborate way like the Fijians, for example. Accounts of battles would mention from time to time that allies in battles had been given a few bodies to eat, but they seem to have specially enjoyed mutilating them to upset their relatives when they found them. The Konso, needless to say, were appalled by the idea of cannibalism, but they did mutilate their dead enemies in battle by castrating them. I discovered this when I was attending a ceremony in the home of a friend, who had just sacrificed a ram to bless his lineage. He took a small piece of the animal's hide, cut a slit in it, and put it on his wrist, telling me as he did so that this is what the Konso used to do with the penises of men they had killed in battle. It is interesting that a castrated man could not be buried on his own land in the normal way, possibly because he was thought to bring sterility to it.

Ours are essentially societies of strangers, living as we do mainly in large cities and even people in villages are always moving from place to place, primarily in relation to where their jobs take them. But in primitive societies people stay in the same place for generations so everyone basically knows everyone else. They know who are the respected and the despised, those with a bad reputation for dishonesty or laziness or being quarrelsome, and the hard workers, the experts and the leaders, the wise heads and the moderators in disputes who make important contributions to the welfare of the group. Our lives are based on the nuclear family, and beyond this blood relationships rapidly fade away, but in primitive societies kinship is a central feature of their lives, and the basis of large groups, not just of isolated families, because people descended from a common ancestor form lineages and clans which are important sources of help in people's daily lives. So people interact with each other not just as individuals but as members of families and lineages and clans, and know who everyone's fathers and grandfathers were, who they married, who their children are and where they live.

It might be thought that members of primitive societies, being illiterate and uneducated, would behave in an uncouth and boorish manner like some of the working class in Western society, but this is quite untrue. The Konso had strict norms of behaviour, enforced by public opinion, while among the Tauade even what we would consider minor insults and slights could result in violent revenge, so people were extremely careful to speak and behave politely. I was interested, however, to see that neither the Konso nor the Tauade said "please" or "thank you", possibly because when constantly interacting with people one knows one takes these exchanges for granted without the need for any special acknowledgement. But I had always assumed that greetings and farewells were human universals, and the Konso certainly used many of these—"Friend!", "Peace today!", "Sleep well!", and so on, but much to my surprise the Tauade had none of them. No one said anything at all when meeting someone else for the first time in the day, and people would join a group in mutual silence. When leaving a man might possibly say "I'm leaving now", but would often go without saying anything. I never ceased to be disconcerted when in the evening I was lighting my stove in my house and talking to someone who was outside on the verandah, and then look up to find that he had silently disappeared into the night. They were very proud and competitive, and perhaps they avoided greetings and farewells because they feared the humiliation of being ignored.

We live in a market economy and have to earn money to buy our food, and need jobs, such as bus-drivers, doctors, civil-servants, firemen, shop-keepers, lawyers, and so on, all of whom have very different life experiences and also status particularly as employers and employees. But in primitive society people produce their own food and so do not need to work for anyone else by selling their labour for money, and their experience of life is far more homogeneous than with us. They simply till their land to grow their crops, and maintain their cattle, sheep, and goats, or their pigs, and killing and eating these is traditionally bound up with social ceremonies, which may involve religious sacrifice, or elaborate exchanges of meat at formal feasts. The only occupations resembling the jobs of our society are specialist craftspeople such as smiths, weavers, and potters, if they exist, but the Tauade didn't even have these, and women knitting string-bags, and in the old days a few men in certain locations making stone tools were about the only crafts.

So, in our society people's identity and social status are intimately tied up with their job as doctor, lawyer, fireman, teacher, plumber, and so on, and also on education and wealth. But in primitive society people mainly get their identity and status from their clan and lineage, their family and especially their father, their gender, their age, whether they are an eldest or a younger son, and the hamlet or village where they live. Since there is no writing or formal schooling there can be no distinction between the educated and the uneducated, though some men will be recognised as more knowledgeable than others. There may also be marked differences of status based on leadership and political skills such mediation, or organizing feasts and dances, bravery in fighting and hunting, and in hard work. But the fact that there is no money, and that people cannot buy or sell their labour, means that status is the basis of such wealth differences as there are, not, as with us, that wealth in money is the basis of social importance. In any case, the poverty of material possessions means that there can be nothing like the huge disparities of material wealth, especially in houses and possessions, that are basic to status differences in our society.

Among advanced farmers like the Konso there may be markets where people can buy necessities like tools, pots, and clothes, but even here money, recently introduced, plays very little part in the rest of daily life. Among the Tauade even markets did not exist, although traditionally men in some villages made stone tools, while the men generally made their own spears and bows and arrows, and the women knitted string bags to carry the produce home from their gardens.

One of the reasons that we encounter so many strangers is not only that we live in large urban communities but that it is so easy for us to get about by all the various means of transportation that are available, and we can also travel in safety. But in primitive societies the only way of getting about, unless there are boats, is on foot along narrow paths, and even more important than the physical difficulties of travel were the dangers of visiting neighbouring groups especially alone, and these dangers only increased with distance. One of the most important effects of law and order imposed by the state has been safety of travel.

It is very strange to live among people who don't measure anything—no rulers, no scales, no thermometers, no calendars, no distances, no weights, no sizes of anything. When it comes to something like house-building the materials are cut by eye and in relation to the human body, not in our manner of blue-prints and standard dimensions. The Tauade were an extreme case of this, as they had no number words beyond "single" and "pair", and they had no means of reckoning time either, beyond a word, *lariata*, for "day". They had no weeks, no months, and no years, and no means of counting them even if they had, so it was impossible to ask them even simple questions like "How long have you been living in this village?", for example. If they wanted to explain when something had happened it would be in relation to some other event, such as "When my father planted those pandanus trees", or "After the Mission came to Kerau". It is perfectly possible, however, to grow crops without any calendar but simply from one's knowledge of the seasons and the weather patterns, and the flowering of different plants. Nor did the Tauade ever try to measure size, or weight, or distance, and this was true of the Konso as well, although they had a well-developed counting system, and the same sorts of words as us like week and month for time-reckoning.

Since there is no form of writing or letters and other types of communication, least of all the variety of electronic communication we have, all human relations have to be face-to-face between real people. Since there are no newspapers all gossip and news, especially from outside the vicinity, is by word of mouth, as are all the traditions and collective memories of the society, and there are no written records to preserve the past.

Without writing there is also no call for any formal schooling—children learn all they need by participating in adult life as they become capable of doing so. In our society, however, school is where children get used to being questioned by their teachers about what they know, or why they think something is true. They are also encouraged to question what they are taught and eventually to develop critical thinking and the ability to reason for themselves. This is all very well where there is literacy and institutions of higher learning, and jobs for engineers, computer-programmers, and professors, but it makes little sense in small non-literate societies with subsistence economies. There "The good child is the obedient child—smartness or brightness by itself is not a highly valued characteristic... wisdom is contrasted with 'cleverness', and wisdom includes good judgement, ability to control people and to keep them at peace, and skill in using speech"[2]. And very sensible, too, one would say, in the context of primitive life. But our emphasis on self-conscious critical thinking and reasoning is one of the foundations of a basic aspect of our culture, which is the huge amount of reflection we engage in about our own thoughts and beliefs and states of mind, and those of other people. But in primitive society this aspect of life, which we can call "reflexive thinking", is largely missing, and it is what people do that matters. In the same way they don't discuss how their own society works and why it is like it is. I once had a conversation with a young man who had had several years at the Mission school, in which I said that the warriors and the elders each had their own kind of work to do in order for the age-system as a whole to work, and he found it very difficult to think along these lines because people are not used to conceptualising the age-system as a working whole; they only know what they as individuals are supposed to do within it.

Again, unlike our society, where churches, scriptures, and formal religious institutions are clearly distinct from what we call "social" institutions like banks and trades unions, in primitive society these merge together, and there is no clear distinction between religion and society. So clans in tribal society are not just social institutions but are often thought of as having a close, "totemic" relationship with species of birds, animals and plants, and their founders and heads are seen as endowed with sacred powers. When I asked the Konso why they had adopted an extremely complicated age-grading system, which regulated the relations between the generations, the standard reply was that "It makes the crops grow", by which they meant that when there was harmony in society, Waqa the Sky God would send rain.

Religious rituals are basically public magic for the health and prosperity of the community, with no concern with beliefs or individual salvation. Members of primitive societies assume they can interact by rituals, words, and actions with the physical world as if it were part of their own social world: they are not focused on a Heavenly world quite different from the world of ordinary experience. And what they want is not individual salvation—they have little interest in the life of the next world, and no idea of Heaven and Hell—but rain, good harvests, children, and good health, with possibly victory in battle against their enemies.

So to understand primitive society we have to think ourselves back from the urban to the rural, where everything is hand-made of local materials, not made by machines in far-away factories, from huge populations to fairly tiny ones, from societies of strangers to societies where everyone more or less knows everyone else as kin or neighbours, from literacy to complete absence of writing, from life dominated by the state and its vast bureaucracy with prisons, police, and a professional army to local communities who have to provide all their own security against external enemies and internal wrong-doers, from relationships dominated by money to relationships where the very idea of money is non-existent, where people are not organized on the basis of a huge range of different jobs, but of kinship, age, and gender which can also be mingled with the sacred so that the symbolic meaning of institutions often takes on profound importance.

2. Talking nonsense about primitive society

Those who have no idea about any of this and want to speculate about early man or human nature in general simply assume that the lives of primitive peoples are basically like ours. For example, someone (Curtis

2013) has recently proposed that "The first, and most ancient function of manners is to solve the problem of how to be social without getting sick [from other people's germs]." The picture of life in the background of this theory is obviously something like modern London, of dense crowds packed into buses and the Tube and breathing each other's germs, shaking hands and kissing, using public lavatories, picking up things other people have handled in shops, and so on. Hunter-gatherer life, at the other extreme, is very healthy: very small populations that cannot support epidemic diseases like measles and small-pox; no domestic animals, especially birds, from which humans can catch a whole range of infections; no clothes or houses which are notorious breeding grounds for a variety of parasites and their diseases; poor communications with other groups and their diseases; and a life in the sun and open air which are powerful antiseptics. If there was a "first and most ancient function of manners" it would actually have been to reduce social friction among small groups of people like this who have to live and get along with one another, not to avoid the largely imaginary dangers from communicable diseases.

Sex at Dawn, (Ryan and Jetha 2010) by a psychologist and his wife, has been enthusiastically received by the general public, particularly by polyamorists. It claims that until 10,000 years ago, hunter-gatherers lived in communities where there was no such thing as marriage, but simply a sexual free-for-all. (They shared everything else, so why not each other?) Then, with the beginning of farming, there also came private property, and this meant that men started to worry about identifying heirs to whom they could pass on their land. This, in turn, produced monogamy and the regulation of our sexual impulses. First of all, it is generally accepted by physical anthropologists that pair-bonding is a key feature of human behavior which separates our species from all other primates, and must go back at least to *Homo erectus*. The elimination of female estrus allowed frequent sexual activity that cemented pair-bonding, and also "reduced the potential for [male] competition and safeguarded the alliances of hunter males" (Wilson

2004: 140-41). Secondly, if their theory were true we would expect to find a sexual free-for-all among existing hunter-gatherers, but marriage is actually a well-attested institution among them—primitive sexual free-for-alls are actually a Victorian myth. And thirdly, farming itself does not normally produce private property, but rather the communal rights of kin-groups over their land, while monogamy, at least as a norm, is far less frequent than polygamy. So, rather a disappointment for the polyamorists after all.

Carrier and Morgan (2014) claim that men's faces and jaws are more robust than women's because for millions of years men have engaged in fist fights just like pub brawls in our society. First of all, in order for natural selection to have produced this result fist fights would have had to be lethal, and we know from bare-knuckle boxing in modern times that they aren't. (Well-known instances of men being killed by a single punch are not the result of the punch but of falling and hitting their heads.) Indeed, where boxing is a social custom it is typically intended as a *non-lethal* form of competition, like wrestling. On the other hand, we know from anthropological studies that when hunter-gatherers (and everyone else) intend serious harm to one another they typically use weapons like clubs, spears, or rocks because they are so much more effective than trying to use one's bare hands, which usually ends up in ineffectual scuffling.

But evolutionary psychologists have probably produced more fanciful theories about early Man than anyone else, and the rest of this chapter will be devoted to them.

(a) The first clothing

It is, of course, true that if we had retained the hairy coats of our primate ancestors we would not need clothes, and we are highly unusual among mammals in lacking effective body hair. Pagel and Bodmer (2003) have proposed that the selective advantage for hairlessness was that it provided freedom from parasites:

*What features of early hominid evolution make hairlessness a plausible response to the toll exacted by parasites? Humans most likely evolved in Africa ... where biting flies and other ectoparasites are found in abundance. Early humans probably lived in close quarters in hunter-gatherer social groups in which rates of ectoparasite transmission were high. Precisely when humans or their hominid ancestors evolved hairlessness must remain a matter of speculation. What we can say is that having fire and the intelligence to produce clothes and shelter, early humans (and possibly even earlier hominids—*Homo erectus *may have had fire) were well equipped to evolve hairlessness as a means of reducing ectoparasitic loads, while avoiding the costs of exposure to sun, cold and rain. Ectoparasites can and do infest clothing, but clothes, unlike fur, can be changed and cleaned.... We suggest, then, that a set of cultural adaptations unique to humans made hairlessness a flexible and advantageous naturally selected adaptation (2003:118).*

They then go on to argue that reduced amounts of body hair may further have been sexually selected for "by virtue of advertising reduced ectoparasitic loads", and so being a desirable trait in a mate (ibid., 118). In fact we haven't the slightest idea what the sexual preferences of *Homo erectus* might have been a million or so years ago, and for all we know the search for lice and fleas in each other's hairy coats might have been an erotically stimulating aspect of courtship[3]. Leaving these speculations on one side, then, we can ask instead if *Homo erectus* might have worn clothing.

When Pagel and Bodmer talk of "clothes" they clearly seem to have in mind some type of woven garment. But people in our society are inclined to take clothes and textiles in general for granted, without realising that woven cloth is an extraordinary achievement, that itself rests on another extraordinary achievement, the ability to spin unlimited quantities of thread. I was myself made vividly aware of the technically difficult and physically arduous process of producing cloth when I lived with the Konso, some of whom were skilled weavers. The thread used was cotton, which first had to be collected from the cotton plants, a tiring process in the fields during the hottest part of the year, and then the seeds had to be removed from the harvested cotton. This involved placing it on a large flat stone and rubbing it vigorously many times with an iron rod, after which the cotton was ready for spinning. The basic tool for producing thread of any kind since the Neolithic has been the spindle, consisting of a rod with a disc, the whorl, of clay or wood at one end to act as a fly-wheel when the spindle is rotated. This was an extremely clever invention which produces an even and compact thread, and before its discovery the basic means of producing thread was by rolling fibres on the thigh, a very inferior technique both in quality and quantity. Konso men, women, and children occupied much of their spare time in spinning, because the production of garments requires an enormous amount of thread, which was sold to the weavers. Their horizontal looms were very complex devices, in which the warp threads were passed through the heddle, operated by the feet, to separate the warp and allow the shuttle to take the weft thread through it. It would take many hours of work to produce a blanket about six feet long and three feet wide. The finished cloth was then sprinkled with chalk and beaten to produce a smooth and even finish.

The Konso Highlands, mostly between 5000 and 6500 feet, have a comfortable temperature somewhere between 65°F and 85°F for most of the year so that physically speaking complete nudity would have been perfectly feasible. (Indeed, in Papua New Guinea the Tauade, where the temperature at 7000 feet could be considerably colder, only wore G-strings as their traditional dress.) So why would the Konso go to all this trouble to weave blankets or even make leather garments? Regardless of climate, one finds that people of most cultures cover the genitals, or at least that the women tend preponderantly to do so, but genital coverings can be made of leaves, or other simple, non-woven materials such as bark-cloth or skins, and do not require any more elaborate form of garment than this. Garments covering large areas of the body, however, are a very different matter, and historically it is clear that the first garments were of sewn skins, and worn by Ice-Age hunters as protection against the cold. On the other hand, hunter-gatherers in tropical latitudes who have been studied in modern times either go completely naked or at most have genital covering. (There are also many reports of people wearing animal skins when sitting in order to keep their backs warm, but beyond this tropical hunter-gatherers do not wear clothes.)

Weaving, as has been pointed out, is a technologically demanding activity quite unsuited to the hunter-gatherer life-style, and even simple forms of finger-weaving on frames, which have been dated as far back as the Gravettian culture of Moldavia at 27,000 BP (from impressions preserved in clay), were still practised in semi-settled conditions, and could only produce simple forms of ornamentation such as sashes and belts, while body garments were made of skins (Soffer et al. 2000). Weaving with looms only appeared with the agricultural revolution in Egypt and similar locations, where it was associated with other crafts such as pottery and metal working, and many different kinds of fibre were used.

It is striking, in view of what we have already established about all the difficulties of producing woven clothes, that highly educated scientists can so casually propose the use of them without even considering what they could have been made of. The suggestion that *Homo erectus* could have had woven garments is preposterous, and it is equally striking that Pagel and Bodmer do not seem to have noticed that hunter-gatherers in tropical climates, which is where our species evolved, don't actually wear any clothes because it is far too hot. Our subsequent ability to produce clothes must therefore be entirely irrelevant to the whole question of hairlessness.

A far more plausible explanation for the evolution of human hairlessness has been provided by Jablonski (2010), who argues that the requirements of a very active hunting life on the African savannah (unique to humans among primates) would have made physiological accommodation to overheating the primary adaptive necessity, and that the human sweating mechanism by evaporation through a naked skin has been demonstrated to be a highly efficient means of dissipating excess heat. So wearing clothes in these conditions would obviously have nullified the whole advantage of nakedness and been highly mal-adaptive.

Parasites make another strange appearance in the history of spec-ulation about the earliest clothes, in the following way. It has been discovered (Kittler, Kayser, & Stoneking 2003) that the body louse evolved from the head louse around 72,000 years BP (plus or minus 42,000 years):

> ...the head louse lives and feeds exclusively on the scalp, whereas the body louse feeds on the body but lives in clothing. This ecological differentiation probably arose when humans adopted frequent use of clothing, an important event in human evolution for which there is no direct archaeological evidence (ibid., 1414).

From this, the science writer Nicholas Wade enthusiastically con-cludes that the ancestral human population that started emigrating out of Africa across the Red Sea around 70,000 years ago must have been wearing tailored clothing: "From the date assigned to the evolution of the human body louse, which lives only in clothing, the ancestral people must have worn clothes that were sewn to fit the contours of the body tightly enough for the lice to feed" (Wade 2007:72). Neither Stoneking and his colleagues, nor Wade, pay any more attention to what these mythical clothes might have been made from than did Pagel and Bodmer, or how they could have been made without first inventing the spindle-whorl and the loom. They also fail to ask themselves the even more obvious question, "Why would anyone in the vicinity of the Red Sea coast, which has always been one of the hottest places on earth with dry season temperatures in excess of 130ºF, even consider laboriously making and then wearing clothes, least of all those that were tightly sewn to their bodies?" They would have been in serious danger of dying from heat-stroke. Tailored clothes of this type are in any case distinctly unusual in pre-modern societies, where garments tend to be made of large pieces of material, like the Konso blanket, the toga, the sari, the kimono, the burnous, and so on. (Tailored clothes began in Europe, for example, when medieval knights needed padded linen undergarments to wear beneath their chain mail, a distinctly specialised requirement.)

These objections from technology and climate seem insurmountable, and I suggested to Professor Stoneking that the use of animal skins as capes and as sleeping skins could have provided an alternative pathway for the body louse. He replied (personal communication): "I think it is quite likely that, as you say, clothing began with humans wearing animal skin capes, and that this is a perfectly plausible mechanism for the origin of body lice: head lice were already adapted to human hair, so it wouldn't have been so difficult to transfer to animal fur/hair, as long as they could continue feeding on the human body". Capes and sleeping skins are well attested in the ethnographic record for hunter-gatherers, they can be used in hot climates, they are technologically very simple, well within the capabilities of early man, and are very likely to be of great antiquity.

(b) The Great Cheating Fiasco

Evolutionary psychologists, in trying to explain the origins of human sociality, have assumed that humans are basically selfish, and are only disposed to behave altruistically to biological kin—"inclusive fitness". They have therefore spilled gallons of ink in discussing the problem of cheating, whose potential advantages to every individual seem a serious obstacle to the development of co-operation. Cosmides and Tooby (1992) provide a splendid example of evolutionary psychologists in full flow on the subject of cheating in their discussion of Trivers" theory of "reciprocal altruism", in which the exchange of benefits between *non-kin* can also be selectively advantageous for both parties concerned.

> *Reciprocal altruism, or social exchange, typically involves two acts: what "you" do for "me" (act 1), and what "I" do for "you" (act 2). For example, you might help me out by baby-sitting my child (act 1), and I might help you out by taking care of your vegetable garden when you are out of town (act 2). Imagine the following the situation: Baby-sitting my child inconveniences you a bit, but this inconvenience is more than compensated for by my watering your garden when you are out of town. Similarly, watering your garden inconveniences me a bit, but this is outweighed by the benefit to me of your baby-sitting my child (1992:171)*

As they say, one might expect natural selection to favour the emergence of this type of behaviour. But, they continue,

> *there is a hitch: You can benefit even more by cheating me. If I take care of your garden, but if you do not baby-sit my child … then you benefit more than if we both cooperate.… Moreover, the same set of incentives applies to me. This single fact constitutes a barrier to the evolution of social exchange.… (ibid., 172).*

While, they admit, it is effectively impossible to cheat if the exchange is simultaneous, as when we give money for the goods that we purchase, "in the absence of a widely accepted medium of exchange, most exchanges are not simultaneous, and therefore do provide opportunities for defection" (ibid., 175) like the baby-sitting/garden-watering defection we first considered. As a consequence they maintain that humans must, during the Pleistocene, have evolved a cognitive "module" of phenomenal complexity (ibid., 177) in order to handle the problem of cheating while still being able to engage in social exchange.

Bearing in mind that we are supposed to be discussing the *evolution* of social exchange among early human beings, the examples of baby-sitting and garden-watering seem remarkably remote from anything our ancestors might plausibly have been doing on the African savannah during the Pleistocene. The whole discussion is utterly disengaged from the actual realities of hunter-gather life, and is, of course, actually centred in our own comfortably familiar WEIRD societies of vast towns full of strangers. In a hunter-gatherer society exchange is actually between people who know each other very well indeed, unlike the suburban baby-sitters and garden-waterers in the example, and is also dominated by *custom*, which leaves very little room for the elaborate calculations so improbably envisaged by Cosmides and Tooby. They are so obsessed with game theory, algorithms, and differential reproduction that they never think for a moment to ask the simple, practical question: "How can people continuously living in very small groups, who have all grown up together and know one another well, who have no money, and who engage in the very basic subsistence tasks of foraging and hunting, actually manage to cheat one another without it being quite obvious?" And even if someone did attempt to cheat it would instantly become known and be greatly to the *disadvantage* of the cheater from the social point of view, regardless of any material benefit.

The basic assumption of evolutionary psychologists that humans are fundamentally selfish is not based on actual evidence but is simply a dogma of neo-Darwinian theory, reinforced by the long tradition of Western individualism and the image of *Homo economicus* rationally striving to maximise his own material interests. In primitive society generally, however one of the most admired virtues is generosity, and one of the most despised vices is meanness. Among the Tauade, who are typical of Papua New Guinea, the lowest social class, the least successful, are the "rubbish-men":

> ...*the* malavi *[rubbish-men] are conventionally considered mean. They are* komutuma, *people who do not give; their bellies are bitter,* lat'logivai, *as opposed to the people who give generously, the* alituma, *especially those who give to children and old people. The* malavi,

*or those who have their nature, are also greedy, and stuff themselves
with food and lick the grease from their hands, and when they have
something, such as tobacco which they should share, take it away to
smoke in private.... A malavi will go and hide in the bush and try
to avoid contributing to feasts in the form of pork or food (Hallpike
1977:144)*

What is completely missing from the ideas of the evolutionary
psychologists is the view of a small *society* as a long-term working entity,
a co-operative endeavour with every individual dependent on his kin
and neighbours As a result the exaggerated importance of cheating in
the society of early hunter-gatherers held by evolutionary psychologists
gets the whole issue back to front. Many years ago I pointed out that
in primitive society generally,

*...the surest method of ensuring social failure and, presumably, some
corresponding decrease in inclusive fitness, is to follow simple strategies
of "selfishness" or "cheating". But human society provides at least
two basic means by which some individuals can enrich themselves
and their relatives at the expense of other members of the group. The
successful person may gain control over some crucial resource such as
land or cattle, or some crucial process, such as political leadership, and
use this as a basis of exploitative relations with dependent individuals,
who are induced to confer more benefits on the dominant individual
than the costs to him of maintaining control over them. Or, the
successful person may have some ability, such as specialized knowledge,
that is valued by the group [e.g shamanism] but is in short supply, and
thereby extract more benefits from the group than the cost of supplying
such services (Hallpike 1984:135).*

Social success in primitive society, therefore, is achieved by those
who are perceived to *help* the group, not by those who cheat and sponge
from it, and cheating as a successful strategy for self-advancement
can only work when a number of basic social changes have taken

place. These are: much larger and more atomistic societies with a high percentage of people who are strangers; the growth of trade and commerce, particularly through the medium of money; the accumulation of material wealth; and the growth of complex bureaucratic systems of redistribution. So it should be obvious that it is not the hunter-gatherer band but modern industrial society that provides by far the most favourable environment for free-loaders to flourish, such as bogus welfare claimants, tax evaders, and confidence-tricksters of every kind, but evolution has sadly neglected to provide us with any "cheater-detection" module to cope with this.

(c) Dialect differences and the threat of strangers

One of the most obvious features of language is how easily dialect differences develop, and unsurprisingly, evolutionary psychologists have an explanation all ready for this:

> *This variability is extremely puzzling given that a universal, unchanging language would seem to be the most useful form of communication. That language has evolved to be parochial, not universal, is surely no accident. Security would have been far more important to early human societies than ease of communication with outsiders. Given the incessant warfare between early human groups, a highly variable language would have served to exclude outsiders and to identify strangers the moment they opened their mouths. Dialects, writes the evolutionary psychologist Robin Dunbar [2003:231], are "particularly well designed to act as badges of group membership that allow everyone to identify members of their exchange group, dialects are difficult to learn well, generally have to be learned young, and change sufficiently rapidly that it is possible to identify an individual not just within a locality but also within a generation within that locality" (Wade 2007:204).*

One might first of all ask just why a universal, unchanging language would be particularly useful in primitive society since, as was historically the case, we only need to speak to the narrow range of people we are likely to meet in real life. Of what conceivable value would it have been, for example, for Aborigines on the east coast of Australia to have been able to converse with those on the west coast, whom they could never have met in the course of many millennia? Secondly, in small-scale primitive societies of hunter-gatherers and early farmers, people *know* who their neighbours are by sight, and if not can easily establish who they are by asking what clan they belong to and where they live. From the point of view of recognising strangers in primitive society, dialect differences are therefore quite superfluous.

Dunbar recognises that "drift", "the gradual accumulation of accidental mutations (mispronunciations, unintended slippages of meaning) over long periods of time" (2003:230) is basically responsible, but cannot accept the obvious fact that this is all the explanation needed because drift would allegedly be too slow: "If the process is not accidental, then it must be deliberate, and deliberate in this context means 'under the influence of selection'. What selection processes could promote such high rates of language change? The most plausible selection pressure is likely to be the need to differentiate communities." And why would this be so important? "*The key problem* [my emphasis] faced by all intensely social organisms that depend on co-operation for successful survival and reproduction is the free-rider—the individual who takes the benefits of co-operation and does not pay the costs." In order for communities to defend themselves against the menace of the free-loader, Dunbar claims to have demonstrated that "a rate of dialect change approaching 50 per cent per generation was required to ensure that individuals who had to exchange resources with each other in order to reproduce were not exploited by free-riders" (ibid., 231).

In the first place, as we saw earlier, the menace of the free-rider that permeates evolutionary psychology is a fantasy. In the simple subsistence economies of hunter-gatherers and early farmers failure to reciprocate in exchange relations, or to participate in communal activities cannot be concealed and got away with. Nor in any case does survival and reproduction have any relation to the *exchange* of resources. The Tauade, who were typical slash-and-burn cultivators of Papua New Guinea, engaged in elaborate exchanges of resources, but this was in fact purely ceremonial and had nothing whatsoever to do with survival or reproduction, since everyone over time received as much as they gave. Everyone knew in detail who everyone else was in these exchanges, back for several generations, because communities were small enough to permit this, and those who failed to meet community standards of generosity in these exchanges were well-known as the "rubbish men" of society, unmarried and certainly with a low rate of reproductive success.

Secondly, if a group's lexicon had a rate of change of 50% per generation this would be obvious in the vocabularies of informants of different age groups, but I never observed any such thing either among the Tauade or the Konso, where my informants ranged from teenage boys to old men. (Modern English is not changing at anything like this rate, of course.) The suggestion that a group would have to produce this rate of linguistic change in order to protect itself from the depredations of free-loaders is quite ridiculous. Nor, for that matter, could natural selection play any part in this. Linguistic change is a *social* phenomenon, like the rate of inflation, not an individual phenomenon, so it cannot in principle be under genetic control, and cannot therefore be selected for.

In conclusion, I would like to return briefly to this notion that the key threat to co-operation in human groups is the free-loading outsider. As I have pointed out again and again, in so far as free-loading is possible at all in such societies it only leads to contempt and low status for those concerned. The Tauade nevertheless did have very major problems with co-operation, but not because they were riddled with free-loading outsiders: if, for example, one asked them why they lived in small hamlets instead of big villages, the standard response was "It is because of our fathers", in other words, festering internal grievances handed down over generations of people who knew each other well. The level of violence and homicide was actually greater *within* local groups than between them (Hallpike 1977:119); the level of violence was greater between adjacent groups on the same side of a river valley (and who interacted frequently), than between groups separated by a river (and who interacted less often); and in the settlement of the Aibala valley it seems clear that a clan who claimed a certain territory first was very ready to invite groups of strangers to come and live there too since this increase of population was both militarily and ceremonially advantageous. It was said that hosts and strangers would exchange sisters in marriage to establish solidarity. The Konso clan and age systems were also designed to be able to assimilate strangers. Strangers, in other words, are not the problem because numbers are generally advantageous; if strangers start to be resented it is because they are thought to be putting too much pressure on scarce resources, not because they are thought to be cheats. It is the people one already knows and dislikes for one reason or another that are always the threat to social cohesion.

(d) The evolution of religion

Evolutionary psychologists have always been fascinated by religion, and discussion of it usually begins something like this: "The propensity for religious belief may be innate because it is found in societies around the world. Innate behaviours are shaped by natural selection because they confer some advantage in the struggle for survival. But if religion is innate, what could that advantage have been?" (Wade 2007:164).

"Religion" is not, in fact, some simple disposition that could usefully be described as innate. It is a highly complex phenomenon both psychologically and culturally, and there are major differences between the forms of religion found in primitive societies and the world religions with which we are familiar, as I have described in detail elsewhere

(Hallpike 1977: 254-74; 2008a: 266-87; 2008b: 288-388; 2016: 62-88). But studying all these ethnographic facts is time-consuming and boring, and it is much more fun to assume that we all know what we mean by "religion"—something like "faith in spiritual beings"—and get on with constructing imaginative explanations about how it must have been adaptive for early man.

"No one", continues Wade, "can describe with certainty the specific needs of hunter-gatherer societies that religion evolved to satisfy. But a strong possibility is that religion co-evolved with language, because language can be used to deceive, and religion is a safeguard against deception. Religion began as a mechanism for a community [wait for it!] *to exclude those who could not be trusted*" [my emphasis] (ibid., 164). And how exactly is this supposed to have worked? The answer is apparently the basic vulnerability of all societies to those free-loaders who are always poised like vultures to take advantage of the system. "Unless free-loaders can be curbed, a society may disintegrate, since membership loses its advantages. With the advent of language, free-loaders gained a great weapon, the power to deceive. Religion could have evolved as a means of defense against free-loading. Those who committed themselves in public ritual to the sacred truth were armed against the lie by knowing that they could trust one another" (ibid., 165).

Now since ritual, myth, and symbolism are fundamental elements of religion in all societies, it is indeed perfectly true that, as embodiments of meaning, they all need some form of linguistic expression in order to be shared in a common culture. For example, the celebrated Hohlenstein-Stadel carving of the Lion Man, a standing male figure with a lion's head, has been dated to 40,000 years BP, and it has been estimated that it took about 400 hours to carve (Cook 2013: 33). It seems inconceivable that anyone could have done all this unless he could also have given some explanation of what he was doing to his companions that they would have understood, and this would obviously have required a reasonably well-developed language.

To this extent Wade is therefore quite correct to claim that "religion" could not have developed without language, but participation in religious ritual has nothing whatever to do with commitment to truth or security against lying. The Konso believed that Waqa, the Sky God, sent rain, indeed that he almost was rain: *Waqa irobini*, "Waqa is raining" was a very common phrase I heard whenever rain fell. He was also believed to withhold rain from villages where there was too much quarrelling, and could strike dead those who lied under a sacred oath. But a crucial difference between the Konso and ourselves is that we are fundamentally aware of the possibility of *unbelief*, of the denial of anything beyond the purely material, so that the assertion of belief in God as *true* in our society is not like the belief of the Konso in Waqa. In their culture there is no real awareness of the possibility of not believing in Waqa, and his reality is simply taken for granted. When Wade says that "religious truths are accepted not as mere statements of fact but as sacred truths, something that it would be morally wrong to doubt" (ibid., 164) this may have some relevance to modern religion, but it has none to the forms of religion in primitive society.

The other selective advantage of religion, according to Wade, is that "It was then co-opted by the rulers of settled societies as a way of solidifying their authority and justifying their privileged position" (ibid., 164). The cynical ruler, smirking behind his hand at the simplicity of the peasants who thought him divine, is actually an invention of the Enlightenment. In fact, in primitive society authority itself attracts sacred status, so that in the traditional society of the Tauade when a Big Man died his body would be put into a specially built enclosure which women were not allowed to enter. Pigs were then slaughtered inside the enclosure and the sacred bull-roarer was whirled, away from the gaze of the women. If enough boys were available they would be kept inside the enclosure in a little hut for several months where they could imbibe the vitality of the dead chief and were taught by adult men to be tough and aggressive. The Big Man's corpse, meanwhile, had been put on a special platform in his hamlet where it was allowed to rot, and it was thought that people absorbed the powers of the Big Man in the smell. Big Men also had a special association with certain birds of prey and sacred oaks, and were believed to be essential for the general health and well being of the group. But these folk beliefs were certainly not "invented" by the Big Men to drum up support.

Again, among the Konso the head of the lineage, the *poqalla*, inherited large amounts of land and was generous to lineage members who needed it with land, stock, and grain, settled disputes between lineage members and represented them in disputes with other lineages. But he was also a sacred figure who was responsible for blessing the members of the lineage and performed annual ceremonies for their health and prosperity; his home was a temporary sanctuary for those who had killed someone; and he was forbidden to attend funerals or visit a home in mourning. Anyone who had been to a funeral had to purify themselves before entering the homestead of the *poqalla*. In some parts of Konso the *poqalla* was also not supposed to kill either in war or hunting, and when they died very special funerals were performed for them. There were also regional *poqalla* who had religious and peacemaking functions for groups of villages. In primitive society, then, authority attracts sacred status which, together with inherited office, is the basis of kingship in later societies.

Rulers and those in authority did not, therefore, in any meaningful sense of the word, "co-opt" religion to justify their privileged position. On the contrary, it was the general human disposition to attribute sacred status to those in authority that was one of the main reasons why it could develop.

(e) Homosexuality and gay uncles

A standing problem in evolutionary psychology is that if there is a substantial genetic basis for homosexuality then how could this have been retained by natural selection, which would inevitably weed out any such disposition to infertility. A classic solution was E.O. Wilson's theory in his *On Human Nature* that homosexuals could have increased their inclusive fitness in foraging bands by assisting their close relatives in child care:

> *The homosexual members of primitive societies could have helped members of the same sex, either while hunting and gathering or in more domestic occupations at the dwelling sites. Free from the special obligations of parental duties, they would have been in a position to operate with special efficiency in assisting close relatives. They might further have taken the roles of seers, shamans, artists, and keepers of tribal knowledge.* If the relatives—sisters, brothers, nieces, nephews, and others—were benefited by higher survival and reproductive rates *[my emphasis], the genes these individuals shared with the homosexual specialists would have increased at the expense of alternative genes. Inevitably, some of these genes would have been those that predisposed individuals toward homosexuality (Wilson 1978:145).*

A study in Samoa purports to provide strong evidence for Wilson's theory.

> Androphilia *refers to sexual attraction and arousal to adult males, whereas* gynephilia *refers to sexual attraction and arousal to adult females. Previous research has demonstrated that Samoan male androphiles (known locally as* fa'afafine*) exhibit significantly higher altruistic tendencies toward nieces and nephews than do Samoan women and gynephilic men. The present study examined whether adaptive design features characterize the psychological mechanisms underlying* fa'afafine's *elevated avuncular tendencies. The association between altruistic tendencies toward nieces and nephews and altruistic tendencies toward nonkin children was significantly weaker among* fa'afafine *than among Samoan women and gynephilic men. We argue that this cognitive dissociation would allow* fa'afafine *to*

allocate resources to nieces and nephews in a more economical, efficient, reliable, and precise manner. These findings are consistent with the kin selection hypothesis, *which suggests that androphilic males have been selected over evolutionary time to act as 'helpers-in-the-nest,' caring for nieces and nephews and thereby increasing their own indirect fitness (Vasey & Vanderlaan 2010).*

In the first place, this study does *not* show that the nieces and nephews of the *fa'afafine* actually benefited from these resources from their uncles so that, as Wilson says, they achieved higher survival and reproductive rates than those without these uncles. Unless this were the case, the homosexual uncles could not have achieved any increase in their inclusive fitness. The Samoan *fa'afafine* is only a special case of what anthropologists know as the avunculate, where the mother's brother has special responsibilities for his sister's children. I actually demonstrated at length (Hallpike 1984) that these gifts of resources in the avunculate relationship were in fact purely ceremonial and could have no effective impact on the life chances of their recipients.

Moreover, the homosexual Samoan *fa'afafine* is a highly unusual institution, and in order to put it in context we need to look at marriage more generally in primitive society, and the first thing we notice is that especially among hunter-gatherers marriage is the norm for everybody. For example,

In Aboriginal Australia generally, the question of whether or not a person should marry does not arise. It is conventionally expected of everyone as a matter of course, and the main problem, who will be selected. A married man is fully, and unquestionably, an adult. Having children confirms his status, even in cases where that is not an acknowledged pre-requisite. And this is so for a woman as well (Berndt & Berndt 1964:166).

This is overwhelmingly the impression given by the literature on other hunter-gatherer societies, and indeed on tribal societies generally.

Girls in particular seem always to be required to marry and may have their spouses selected for them, and the pressure on men is almost equal. I never encountered a woman either among the Konso or the Tauade who had not married, although one Konso woman had been rejected by her husband because she was barren. Among the Konso the only men who did not marry were the *sakoota*, who were clearly rather effeminate, wore skirts, practised female crafts and were thoroughly despised. They were a tiny proportion of the population, a fraction of one percent, and were a source of shame to their kin, certainly not benevolent gay uncles. Among the Tauade there was also a class of unmarried men, the "rubbish-men" who are a standard New Guinean institution like the Big Man. But I never heard any suggestion that they were homosexual, but were simply social inadequates that no woman would consider marrying. Indeed, when I asked my main informant Amo Lume about homosexuality he had to think hard before he recalled one man who had liked to wear a European dress after these began to be imported. But that was the only example he could think of, and I could find no references to homosexuality among the Tauade either in their myths or in local court cases or any of the patrol reports.

Ford and Beach (1951), in their cross-cultural survey of sexual practices and attitudes, report that of the seventy-six societies for which information was available for their survey, in twenty-eight of them homosexual activities between adults were either absent or very rare. In the remaining forty-nine, homosexual activities were acceptable for certain members of the community, and the commonest of these was similar to the Konso *sakoota*, or *berdache* as the role is commonly known, and might often be a shaman and ascribed magical powers:

Among the Siberian Chukchee such an individual puts on women's clothing, assumes female mannerisms, and may become the "wife" of another man. The pair copulate per anum, *the shaman always playing the feminine role. In addition to the shaman "wife", the husband usually has another wife with whom he indulges in heterosexual coitus. The shaman in turn may support a feminine mistress; children are often born of such unions (Ford & Beach 1951: 130-31).*

But homosexuality in tribal societies most frequently involves adolescent boys, not gay uncles:

> *Among the Siwans of Africa, for example, all men and boys engage in anal intercourse. They adopt the feminine role only in strictly sexual situations and males are singled out as peculiar if they do not indulge in these homosexual activities" (ibid., 131-32)... Among many of the Aborigines of Australia this type of coitus is a recognized custom among unmarried men and uninitiated boys. Strehlow writes of the Aranda as follows: '...Pederasty is a recognized custom.... Commonly a man, who is fully initiated but not yet married, takes a boy of ten or twelve years old, who lives with him as a wife for several years, until the older man marries'... Keraki bachelors of New Guinea universally practice sodomy, and in the course of his puberty rites each boy is initiated into anal intercourse by the older males. After his first year of playing the passive role he spends the rest of his bachelorhood sodomizing the newly initiated. This practice is believed by the natives to be necessary for the growing boy" (ibid., 132). (In due course the boys marry in the usual way.)*

Wilson's hypothesis of the helpful, nepotistic homosexual uncle increasing his inclusive fitness by looking after his nieces and nephews does not, then, find any ethnographic support, and his ideas are in fact completely uninformed speculation. Even accepting that there are genes disposing people to homosexuality, Wilson's basic fallacy is very simple: he assumes, quite wrongly, that homosexuals can't (or won't) marry and have children, whereas there is plenty of evidence from anthropology, the classical world, and more recent history, that homosexuals of both genders are quite capable, in most cases, of marrying and begetting children. Given the enormous social pressures for marriage in traditional societies, it is far simpler than Wilson's scenario, and more in accordance with the known facts, merely to assume that if these genes for homosexuality exist, they were perpetuated by those with homosexual inclinations who nevertheless married and begot children, thereby making their "homosexual" genes invisible to natural selection.

Notes

1. Haidt 2012: 96.
2. Taken from Wober 1974: 271.
3. Dunbar maintains that it was actually highly adaptive to have hairy coats full of parasites, because they provided an opportunity for grooming which was a major factor in strengthening social bonds, as it is with apes:

> *Dunbar (1996)…claims a unique pressure for human ancestors [to develop language]: the growth of groups to a size too large to allow time for the grooming that forms a vital part of primate interactions. But other arguments render this implausible. There is no evidence that human groups grew larger than ape groups until quite recently, indeed what little evidence there is points in the opposite direction. Baboon groups are substantially larger than ape groups, yet no grooming substitute has developed among them. No valid reason is given for why meaningless, soothing sounds would not have functioned as well (or better) as a grooming device than a more complex adaptation that required every utterance to have some sort of propositional meaning. The sole function claimed by Dunbar— gossip—could not have been exercised until language acquired a critical mass of at least several hundred words, for in its earliest stages its symbols were presumably enumerable in the single digits, and how many items of gossip could you convey with a single set of nine words? For language to enter the repertoire of human behavior, it had to convey an adaptive advantage from its very earliest stages, or it would never have fixed.(Bickerton 2007: 514-15)*

A response to *Swearing is Good for You. The amazing science of bad language*, by Emma Byrne

Most of us, when confronting some particularly obstinate piece of DIY, know the satisfaction of letting rip with some fruity swear-words, so it is reassuring to learn that laboratory experiments confirm that swearing really does diminish sensations of pain. But Byrne's thesis is more important than merely showing that swearing can be beneficial in various ways, since she argues that swearing has been an integral part of human evolution, especially in the development of language, from ancient to modern times:

> It's my hypothesis that swearing started early, that it was one of the things that motivated us to develop language in the first place. In fact, I don't think we would have made it as the world's most populous primate if we hadn't learnt to swear. As we've seen, swearing helps us deal better with our pain and frustration, it helps us to build tighter social groups and it's a good sign that we might be about to snap, which means that it forestalls violence. Without swearing, we'd have to resort to the biting, gouging and shit flinging that our primate cousins use to keep their societies in check. (Byrne 2017: 119)

Dr Byrne is a neuroscientist and a specialist in artificial intelligence, but unfortunately has no knowledge of anthropology that would have been rather useful in relation to her chosen topic. As a result the vast majority of her examples are drawn from the Anglosphere and

Western culture in general, and far too little attention is given to non-Western cultures: Japan, for example, which apparently "suffers" from an almost complete lack of swearing, deserves a whole chapter to itself. But Westerners are always making the ethnocentric assumption that what is normal for them must also be normal for everyone else, a constant and universal feature of human nature itself, whereas in fact it may just be a product of social and cultural factors, and I shall try to show that this is the case with swearing.

Before we discuss Byrne's theory in detail, however, we should briefly review the basic features of swearing. In many cultures people deliberately use certain words, known to us as "swear-words", that would normally be considered offensive, in order to add force to what they are saying ("intensifiers"), or as insults, or to express frustration or pain. It should be noted, however, that not all insults are swear-words—"liar", "scum", or "thief", for example—nor are many intensifiers—"fantastic", "amazing" and so on. Cross-culturally, we find that by far the commonest criteria of offensive and insulting language are references to excretion of all kinds, the sexual parts and behaviour, especially in relation to a person's mother or other near relatives, and blasphemy. (It is ironic that the basic and original meanings of "swear" and "oath" are the highly respectable contexts of justice and religion, as when witnesses in court swear on oath to tell the truth "so help me God". They only acquired their more common and opposite meanings when people "took the Lord's name in vain" and indulged in profanity ("violating the sacred") and cursing.)

The first essential feature of swear-words is therefore that they should refer to some particular subject-matter that has shock value deriving from violation of various taboos. As we have noted, the commonest of these taboos are sexual matters, followed by those related to excretion, and in many cultures blasphemy is also an important taboo. In an immense range of cultures notions of pollution centre on certain bodily states—excretion, sexuality, menstruation, birth, eating and death—and one might say that the archetypal image of dirt is that of faeces.

Certainly the original meaning of English "dirt" was Middle English *drit*, "ordure", "excrement". But while disgust at faeces is a cultural universal, disgust in itself is not sufficient to generate swear-words. Pus, vomit, and decomposing flesh are also disgusting but play a minimal part in the vocabulary of swearing, while the human genitals in and of themselves are not considered disgusting at all, nor is sexual intercourse. So we should be clear that the notion of pollution is not based narrowly on disgust, and the central meaning of impurity or "dirt" has plausibly been said to be "the organic aspect of man" (Dumont 1970: 50), "the irruption of the biological into social life" (Parker 1990: 63). All this goes to show that in swearing we are dealing with complex cultural categories, not with simple psychological reactions like anger, frustration, or hostility.

Secondly, and equally important, the culture must also distinguish in some way between types of words that are considered coarse, as opposed to polite or formal, and have conventions about when each type of word is permissible. The shock is delivered by using a "coarse" word in a polite context, whereas using a "polite" word with an excretory or sexual meaning simply doesn't work as a swear-word—"excrement-head" instead of "shit-head" for example. Thirdly, social context is crucial in determining whether a coarse word is actually liable to cause offence: a group of men or workmates as opposed to mixed company or where children are present, a private conversation as opposed to an official meeting, speech as opposed to writing, and so on. So while swearing clearly gives various types of psychological satisfaction it can only work in a particular type of culture with taboos and an appropriate vocabulary.

We can now move on to consider Byrne's theory about the necessity of swearing in the emergence of language. Since it is obvious at the outset that we have no evidence at all for how language developed among early human groups, and what they may have talked about, Byrne's belief that swearing must have been an essential part of the process has to look elsewhere for support. As she puts it:

If we can't observe the development of swearing directly, what we need is a society with brains and social structures somewhat like our own, but that are only just beginning to use language. Thankfully, at least one example does exist, in the shape of the chimpanzees who have been taught to use sign language over the years. (p.120)

She is referring to the studies of chimpanzees carried out in particular by the well-known Washoe project run by the Gardners, and at the Chimpanzee and Human Communication Institute in Washington by Professor Roger Fouts. It is very important to note, however, that these animals were not in their wild state, but reared in Western homes, and since chimpanzees do not have the vocal apparatus for human speech, Washoe and the other apes including those trained by Professor Fouts were taught American Sign Language, and we may accept that they were able to produce strings of a few signs to communicate with their human guardians in rudimentary ways. To describe these chimpanzees, however, as "a society with brains and social structures somewhat like our own, but that are only just beginning to use language" is more than a little wide of the mark. A few chimpanzees living in a human household do not constitute a "society" of any recognizable type, and certainly not one in any way resembling the foraging bands of early man; after five million years of evolution chimpanzee brains are in many ways significantly different from our own (ours are three times larger for a start), and most linguists would deny that the chimpanzees in question were actually beginning to use language in the sense of acquiring grammar.

It is of special importance in assessing this attempt to simulate early human society to note that in order to live in a human household, as distinct from remaining in the wild, the chimpanzees obviously had to be toilet-trained, and were made to understand that doing their business anywhere but in the potty was BAD and DIRTY. "Among Washoe and the other chimpanzees raised by the Gardners and their team, the DIRTY sign was consistently used by chimpanzees and humans alike for faeces, dirty clothes and shoes, and for bodily functions" (p.137). It is the crucial sign that Byrne claims links the chimpanzees with swearing. Not perhaps surprisingly, the DIRTY sign also became used as an insult "when people or other animals did not do what Washoe wanted. This wasn't something Washoe was taught to do; she spontaneously began using DIRTY as a pejorative and as an exclamation whenever she was frustrated" (p.137). Byrne admits, however, that this use of DIRTY was the result of the intensive potty-training that they were given by the human experimenters, and the same seems to have been the case with Fouts' chimpanzees who used the DIRTY sign in the same way. Wild chimpanzees will throw faeces when angry, as they will any other convenient object, but they are not reported as treating faeces as especially offensive, and defecation is evidently considered a normal function like eating. So it should be obvious that the association between excretion and something dirty was not one that the chimpanzees made spontaneously, all by themselves, and was one that they would surely never have made in the wild.

Again, while DIRTY as used in the Washoe programme was about faeces, among other things such as clothes and shoes, it did not itself specifically denote faeces and was a perfectly respectable sign, unlike SHIT in our vocabulary. (This also appears to apply to Fouts' experiments as well.) While DIRTY may have been an expression of anger, dislike, or frustration it was therefore not really swearing at all, any more than we are swearing when we angrily describe some item of pornography as "sheer FILTH". Byrne provides no evidence that the animals used sexual or scatological signs either as abuse or as exclamations of pain or frustration. It must also be emphasised that Byrne says nothing at all about signs referring to sexuality and the genitals in the chimpanzees' training either, but sexual modesty, like excretory modesty, is not found among wild chimpanzees or bonobos, and while junior male chimpanzees may conceal their copulation from alpha males, this is merely from fear of reprisals. In human society, however, sexual modesty is a cross-cultural universal, as to a considerable extent excretory modesty is also. Where then might early humans have got the idea that sex and excretion were "dirty" in the first place, since this association is unknown to animals? Even the evolutionary psychologist must surely falter when asked how potty-training could have worked among our ancient ancestors. It would seem then that the idea that excretion and sex are dirty could only have been communicated by some sort of language, which must therefore already have existed, and that swearing must if anything have been a consequence and not a cause of this process.

But even if our ancient ancestors had had the notion that excretory and sexual matters were in some sense dirty or taboo, it seems im-plausible that, at the very beginning of their experience with language, they could also have simultaneously developed a distinctively "coarse" vocabulary in which to refer to them. Let us, however, assume for argument's sake that swearing has always throughout history been an essential part of human language and conversation. If this were so then we would obviously expect to find it in every society, particularly primitive society, but this is not the case. So when I lived among the Konso of Ethiopia (1965-67) and the Tauade of Papua New Guinea (1970-72), I discovered that they did not swear at all, in our sense of "What the f*ck?", "A shitty day", "A piss-poor effort", and so on. This was simply because they had no swear-words whatever: the words they used for faeces, sexual intercourse, penis, vagina, and so on were at the same level of propriety as the words for house, tree, pot, woman, and so on. In simple cultures of this type there is no such thing as a slang or "coarse" vocabulary that is distinct from a proper or formal or polite one. So it would have been quite bizarre for a Konso man to say *suda*, "sexual intercourse", if he dropped a rock on his toe, and his response would actually have been a cry of pain, something like "Aieee!" It is therefore impossible in these societies to use what we may call "biological" words with the necessary shock value to intensify speech in the way that we do when swearing. Intensification of speech is achieved simply by emphasis and intonation.

The Konso and the Tauade seem in fact to be typical of primitive societies—small-scale, non-literate, societies based on kinship, gender and age, without political centralisation or money—in lacking swearing in our sense of the word. In the 888 cultural categories listed in the Outline of Cultural Materials published by the Human Relations Area Files (Murdock et al. 1961), a world-wide survey primarily concerned with primitive societies, there is no category concerned with swearing, and it does not occur in the indexes of the many ethnographies from various parts of the world in my own library. Bergen (2016) in his survey of swearing cited by Byrne does not mention any primitive societies either, and while it is notoriously hard to prove a negative it seems reasonable to conclude that swearing is not a primordial human trait at all, but a relatively late cultural development. This may be associated with literate society in particular, because these societies are especially likely to develop distinctions between "coarse" and "polite" discourse and enforce sexual and excretory modesty with particular severity. Blasphemy, too, which is a fertile source of swearing, is not a cross-cultural universal either. It could not exist among the Tauade because their only supernatural beings were evil spirits whom it would have been pointless and probably dangerous to abuse, and ancient culture heroes at the beginning of time who had turned to stone long ago. Waqa was the Sky-God of the Konso, who was a moral deity who punished sinners and sent the rain to the good, so that it would have been unthinkable for them to blaspheme his name and I never heard of anyone doing so. It would seem that blasphemy is more likely to develop in literate societies with official priesthoods and formal religious institutions.

The absence of swear-words did not mean that either among the Tauade or the Konso one could talk about sexual matters as freely as anything else. On the contrary, it was considered most improper to refer to them when in the homestead, or in mixed company. While the unmarried Konso girls could joke harmlessly with me when I first arrived about which of them I would marry, I once accidentally said the word for "vagina" when one of them was standing near me, and she hurried off very quickly. It is not therefore the vocabulary itself that is inherently offensive, but the context in which it is used.

Insult, however, is quite a different matter from swearing because here the whole purpose is to give offence, and it is not necessary to use swear-words in order to do so, although of course they are extremely useful for this. Among the Tauade and the Konso we do indeed find the same basic taboos concerning sex and excretion as seem to occur all over the world. Among the Tauade, for example (Hallpike 1977: 248), the typical insults were of the following types, using standard vocabulary in each case:

- Eat my/your faeces

- Eat my/your pig's/dog's faeces

- Lick my/your wife's vagina/anus

- Drink my/your husband's semen/urine

- Come and copulate with my/your pig

And among the Konso the standard imprecation, particularly among the boys, was "Your mother's vagina".

The only other possible function of swearing in groups of early man might have been as a form of social bonding. Byrne notes the very common use of swear-words among small groups of people who know each other well, often as teams of co-workers. We can agree with her that swearing functions here as an important aspect of joking relationships, and the mutual tolerance of what would otherwise be insulting or indecent language is actually a token of the group's solidarity: "We like each other far too much to take offence". But we have no particular reason to suppose that these conditions could have applied among the small groups of early Man in the initial stages of language development. These small groups do not develop the necessary distinction between "coarse" and "polite" vocabularies, and if we consider social relations in modern-hunter-gatherer bands, as reported by anthropologists, they do not seem to be of the type that would easily tolerate jocular insults at all.

While one might expect forager bands to be tightly knit groups rather like teams of co-workers in our society, the reality is clearly very different, one of considerable mutual indifference and even some social tension and unease. So Whiting cites a cross-cultural study of child-rearing by Barry, Child and Bacon (1959) which found that foraging cultures tend to stress assertiveness and independence rather than the compliance which is typical of agricultural and pastoral norms (1968: 37). Marshall says of the !Kung, "Altruism, kindness, sympathy, or genuine generosity were not qualities that I observed often in their behaviour" (1976: 350). Howell observes of the Chewong of Malaysia, "Although they do not compete, they do not help each other either.... It is a rare sight to witness someone asking someone else for assistance. Similarly, offers of assistance are also rare (1989: 30). Holmberg says of the Siriono, "Unconcern for one's fellows is manifested on every hand" (1969: 260), and Gardener says of the Paliyans that they "work and live in parallel rather than in joint fashion and exhibit little cooperation outside their rather loose nuclear families" (1966: 394). Woodburn says that "The Hadza are strikingly uncommitted to each other; what happens to the individual Hadza, even close relatives, does not really matter very much" (1968: 91). And Balikci says of the Netsilik Eskimo that their bands were permeated by suspicion and hostility: "Practically any minor or trivial event could produce a quarrel and lead to overtly aggressive behaviour" (1970: 173). In these types of society swearing would not forestall violence but would be much more likely to provoke it, and hunter-gatherers have perfectly effective means of preserving the peace, such as gift-exchange, public ridicule, ostracism, and mutual avoidance.

It seems likely that a major reason for this relative lack of solidarity is that hunter-gatherer bands do not regularly interact with other bands, so that group solidarity is not a very relevant value. In pastoral and agricultural societies, however, with much larger populations, these are divided into groups which do have to interact constantly with each other, such as lineages, residential groups within settlements, age-groups, and working parties, and these sorts of groups do indeed tend to have strong norms of friendliness and co-operation between their members. For example, I was once sitting with a group of Konso men who were digging the grave for one of their ward members who had just died, and among whom just these norms of friendliness and co-operation applied. Grave-digging is carried out by neighbours, not kinsfolk, and the dead man's family give them liberal quantities of beer, so these are actually very social occasions with plenty of laughing and joking. They were asking me if we had lions, or elephants, or leopards, or rhinos in England, to which I had repeatedly to answer "No". Finally, exasperated by this, the grave-digger, who was working naked to preserve his cotton shorts, pointed to his penis and said "Do you have these in England?", and we all fell about laughing. If this had occurred in one of the public assembly places, especially with women present, it would have been considered highly indecent, but in a friendly group of men it did indeed work as a form of joking relationship and enhance solidarity. Again, a group of men and boys would often gather in the doorway of my hut in the evening, and if one of them broke wind we would play the game of "Who's the farter?", where one of the men would pull some straws from the thatch and the boy who drew the short straw would be given a good-natured pummeling.

To sum up, therefore, joking about tabooed subjects like sex and excretion among single sex groups especially may have been a social lubricant from the most ancient of times, but swearing needs at least three conditions: tabooed subjects, a special coarse vocabulary to refer to them that is considered impolite, and a willingness to tolerate its use on certain occasions or situations. The second and third of these conditions are missing in many primitive societies in particular, so it seems fair to conclude that swearing is highly unlikely to have featured in the conversation of our early ancestors and been an essential stimulus of language, or to have been a constant phenomenon throughout history. On the contrary, far from being an ancient relic of our Palaeolithic past, it appears to have been a much later product of social and cultural complexity.

Review of Yuval Harari's *Sapiens: A Brief History of Humankind*

The biological title *Sapiens* is intended to give the impression of a work of hard-nosed science in the Darwinian tradition. Human history is presented as "the next stage in the continuum of physics to chemistry to biology", and our ultimate destiny, and not so very ultimate either, is to be replaced by intelligent machines. It is a summary of human cultural and social evolution from stone age foraging bands through the agricultural revolution, writing and the rise of the state and large-scale societies, through the gradual process of global unification through empires, money, and the world religions, to the scientific revolution that began the modern world and its consequences.

As an anthropologist who has trodden roughly the same path as Harari in a number of books (Hallpike 1979, 1986, 2008, 2016) I was naturally curious to see what he has to say, but it soon became clear that its claim to be a work of science is questionable, beginning with his notion of culture. Language is obviously the basis of human culture, but one of the central themes of the book is the idea that not just language but what he calls "fiction" has been crucial in the ascent of Man:

> *[T]he truly unique feature of our language is not its ability to transmit information about men and lions. Rather it's the ability to transmit information about things* that do not exist at all *[my emphasis]. As far as we know, only Sapiens can talk about entire kinds of entities that they have never seen, touched or smelled.... But fiction has*

enabled us not merely to imagine things, but to do so collectively. *We can weave common myths such as the biblical creation story, the Dreamtime myths of Aboriginal Australians, and the nationalist myths of modern states. Such myths give Sapiens the unprecedented ability to cooperate flexibly in large numbers. (27)*

The claim that culture is *fiction* is not an important insight, but is simply a perverse way of stating the obvious fact that culture is a set of shared ideas, and ideas by their very nature can't be material objects. Language has been revolutionary because it has allowed human beings to be linked together by shared ideas into roles and institutions. One cannot *see* or *touch* the Prime Minister, for example, but only a human being, and someone who does not know what "Prime Minister" *means* has to be told. This can only be done properly by explaining how this role fits into the British Constitution, which in turn involves explaining parliament, cabinet government, the rule of law, democracy, and so on. This world of roles, institutions, beliefs, norms, and values forms what we call culture, but just because the components of culture are immaterial and cannot be seen, touched or smelled does not make them *fiction*, like Santa Claus and the Tooth Fairy, or the myths of Genesis or the Australian Aborigines. We can't see, touch, or smell truth because truth is not a material object, but that does not make it unreal or fictitious either.

If Harari's test of reality is only what we can see, touch, or smell, then mathematics, like truth, should also be a prime example of fiction. Maybe simple integers might just pass his reality test, since we can see groups of different numbers of things, but how "real" in his sense are zero, negative numbers, irrational numbers like π or imaginary numbers like the square root of -1? And if mathematics is fiction, then so is the whole of science including the theory of relativity and Darwinian evolution, which Harari would find very embarrassing indeed because he loves science. He is just in a philosophical muddle that confuses what is material with what is real, and what is immaterial with fiction.

But the opposite of fiction is not what is material but what is true, and what is fictional and what is true can both only exist in the immaterial world of thought.

When it comes to the task of explaining social institutions, the idea of culture as fiction is about as useful as a rubber nail:

> *People easily understand that "primitives" cement their social order by believing in ghosts and spirits, and gathering each full moon to dance together round the campfire. What we fail to appreciate is that our modern institutions function on exactly the same basis. Take for example the world of business corporations. Modern business-people and lawyers are, in fact, powerful sorcerers. (31)*

Really? He takes the Peugeot motor company, with its image of a lion, and tries to argue that the company itself is no more real than an ancient tribal totem, but nevertheless can form the basis on which large numbers of people could co-operate:

> *How exactly did Armand Peugeot, the man, create Peugeot, the company? In much the same way that priests and sorcerers have created gods and demons throughout history.... It all revolved around telling stories, and convincing people to believe them.... In the case of Peugeot SA the crucial story was the French legal code, as written by the French parliament. According to the French legislators, if a certified lawyer followed all the proper liturgy and rituals, wrote all the required spells and oaths on a wonderfully decorated piece of paper, and affixed his ornate signature to the bottom of the document, then hocus pocus—a new company was formed. (34)*

Harari seems unable to distinguish a belief from a convention, presumably because neither is a material object. Beliefs in ghosts and spirits may be shared by members of particular cultures, but derive from the nature of people's experience and their modes of thought: they did not sit down and deliberately agree to believe in them. Conventions, however, are precisely the result of a collective decision, consciously taken to achieve a certain purpose, and as such are completely different from myths in almost every respect. Peugeot SA rests on the legal convention of a limited-liability company, which performs a very useful social function, and another very useful social convention is the rule of the road by which in Britain we all drive on the left. Neither beliefs in spirits nor social conventions are material objects, but they are still quite different sorts of thing, as are legal documents and magical rituals, and Harari achieves nothing by confusing them.

More unsustainable claims do not take long to appear. It may well be true that by about 400,000 years ago Man became able to hunt large game on a regular basis, and that in the last 100,000 years we jumped to the top of the food chain. There also seems little doubt that after humans migrated out of Africa in the last 70,000 years or so they exterminated large mammals in Australia, the Americas, and other parts of the world. But part of his explanation for this is that:

> *Having so recently been one of the underdogs of the savannah, we are full of fears and anxieties over our position, which makes us doubly cruel and dangerous. Many historical calamities, from deadly wars to ecological catastrophes, have resulted from this over-hasty jump. (12-13)*

No, we're not full of fears and anxieties about our position in the food chain, and never have been, because a species is not a person who can remember things like having been the underdog of the savannah tens of millennia in the past. Knowledge of our life on the savannah has only been vaguely reconstructed by archaeologists and anthropologists in modern times.

He then describes us as "embarrassingly similar to chimpanzees" and claims that:

> *Our societies are built from the same building blocks as Neanderthal or chimpanzee societies, and the more we examine these building*

blocks—sensations, emotions, family ties—the less difference we find
between us and other apes. (42)

In fact, however, if we study the research on the differences between
human infants and chimpanzees, such as Tomasello's *Why We Co-*
operate (2009), the *greater* we find the differences between us and other
apes. Tomasello's studies of pre-linguistic human infants between 12–
24 months and chimpanzees showed marked differences in behaviour
related to co-operation, for example. Human infants start co-operating
at about 12 months, and when 14–18 month infants were put in
situations where adult strangers needed help with problems, the infants,
unlike chimpanzees, spontaneously provided it. Even before speech develops human infants will try to provide information to adult strangers
who need it by pointing, whereas apes do not understand informative
pointing at all. Infants also have an innate grasp of rules, in the sense
of understanding that certain sorts of activities, like games, should be
done in a certain way, whereas apes do not. 14–24 month old infants
also collaborate easily in social games, whereas chimpanzees simply
refuse to take part in them, and infants can also change and reverse roles
in games. Human collaborative activity is achieved through generalised
roles that can potentially be filled by anyone, including the self. This is
the basis of the unique feature of human culture, the institution, which
is a set of practices governed by rules and norms. "No animal species
other than humans has been observed to have anything even vaguely
resembling [social institutions]." (Tomasello 2009: xi–xii).

For Harari the great innovation that separated us from the apes was
what he calls the Cognitive Revolution, around 70,000 years ago when
we started migrating out of Africa, which he thinks gave us the same
sort of modern minds that we have now. "At the individual level,
ancient foragers were the most knowledgeable and skilful people in
history.... Survival in that area required superb mental abilities from
everyone" (55), and "The people who carved the Stadel lion-man some
30,000 years ago had the same physical, emotional, and intellectual

abilities we have" (44). Not surprisingly, then, "We'd be able to explain to them everything we know—from the adventures of Alice in Wonderland to the paradoxes of quantum physics—and they could teach us how their people view the world" (23).

It's a sweet idea, and something like this imagined meeting actually took place a few years ago between the linguist Daniel Everett and the Piraha foragers of the Amazon in Peru (Everett 2008). But far from being able to discuss quantum theory with them, he found that the Piraha couldn't even count, and had no numbers of any kind. They could teach Everett how they saw the world, which was entirely confined to the immediate experience of the here-and-now, with no interest in past or future, or really in anything that could not be seen or touched. They had no myths or stories, so Alice in Wonderland would have fallen rather flat as well.

Harari's belief that the Cognitive Revolution provided the modes of thought and reasoning that are the basis of our scientific civilisation could not therefore be further from the truth. We may accept that people became able to speak in sentences at this time, and language is certainly essential to human culture, but anthropologists and developmental psychologists, in their studies of primitive societies, have found that their language development and their modes of thought about space, time, classification, causality and the self have much more resemblance to those of the Piraha than to those of members of modern industrial societies. The Piraha are an extreme case, but the Tauade of Papua New Guinea with whom I lived, for example, only had the idea of single and pair, and no form of calendar or time-reckoning. Harari clearly has no knowledge at all of cross-cultural developmental psychology, and of how modes of thought develop in relation to the natural and socio-cultural environments. The people who carved the Stadel lion-man around 30,000 years ago and the Piraha had the same ability to *learn* as we do, which is why Piraha children can learn to count, but these cognitive skills have to be learnt: we are not born with them all ready to go. Cross-cultural developmental psychology has shown that the development of the cognitive skills of modern humans actually requires literacy and schooling, large-scale bureaucratic societies and complex urban life, the experience of cultural differences, and familiarity with modern technology, to name some of the more important requirements (see Hallpike 1979).

While Harari recognises that we know almost nothing about the beliefs and social organization of ancient foragers, he agrees that the constraints of their mode of life would have limited them to small-scale groups based on the family without permanent settlements (unless they could fish), and with no domestic animals. But then he launches into some remarkable speculations about what they might nevertheless have achieved in the tens of thousands of years between the Cognitive Revolution and the beginning of agriculture.

> *These long millennia* may have witnessed *[my emphasis] wars and revolutions, ecstatic religious movements, profound philosophical theories, incomparable artistic masterpieces.... The foragers may have had their all-conquering Napoleons who ruled empires half the size of Luxembourg; gifted Beethovens who lacked symphony orchestras but brought people to tears with the sound of their bamboo flutes....*
> *(68-9)*

Er, no. They couldn't. All these imagined triumphs of the hunter-gatherers would actually have required a basis of large populations, centralized political control and probably literate civilisation, which in turn would have required the development of agriculture.

This is normally regarded as, after language, the innovation that made possible the extraordinary flowering of human abilities. As Harari correctly points out, agriculture developed independently in a number of parts of the world, and tribal societies based on farming became extremely common, many of them surviving into modern times. But he describes the Agricultural Revolution as "history's biggest fraud" because individuals in fully developed farming societies generally had an inferior diet and harder work than foragers, and their food supply depended on a limited range of crops that were vulnerable to drought, pests, and invaders, unlike the more varied food resources of hunter-gatherers. These criticisms of agriculture are, of course, quite familiar, and up to a point legitimate. But if agriculture was really such a bad deal why would humans ever have gone along with it? Harari begins by suggesting that wheat and other crops actually domesticated us, and made us work for them, rather than the other way round, but this doesn't get him very far in explaining the persistence of agriculture, and instead he argues that wheat offered nothing to individuals, but only to the species by enabling the growth of larger populations. But since it is actually individuals who have to do all the hard work of sowing and reaping this won't do either, so finally he says that people persisted in the agricultural way of life because they were in search of an easier life, and couldn't anticipate the full consequences of agriculture.

> Whenever they decided to do a bit of extra work—say, to hoe the fields instead of scattering the seeds on the surface—people thought, "Yes, we will have to work harder, but the harvest will be so bountiful! We won't have to worry any more about lean years. Our children will never go to sleep hungry." It made sense. If you worked harder, you would have a better life. That was the plan. (97)

It didn't work out that way, however, because people didn't foresee population growth, poor diet and disease. Since it would have taken many generations to realise all the disadvantages of agriculture, by that time the population would have grown so large that it would have been impossible to go back to foraging, so the agricultural trap closed on Man for evermore.

The change from foraging to agriculture as principal mode of subsistence would have actually taken hundreds of years in many cases, and there are many important advantages of agriculture which he ignores. It is likely that one of the primary attractions of planting crops was that it allowed people to live in fixed settlements for some or all of the year, for a variety of reasons. Some favoured locations would have provided access to a plentiful supply of food or water; a whole series of craft activities are all more conveniently carried out in permanent or semi-permanent settlements; and these are also very convenient for holding ceremonies such as initiations and feasts. We also know that the food surplus from agriculture can be used in systems of exchange and competitive feasting, for trading with different groups, and for feeding domestic animals. A larger population also has many attractions in itself: it permits a much richer social life than is possible for small foraging bands, with more impressive ceremonies, a larger labour force for social projects such as irrigation and communal buildings, and more effective defence against local enemies. Agriculture would therefore have had many attractions which would have been obvious to the people concerned (see Hallpike 2008: 52-65).

Agriculture with the domestication of animals, then, was the essential foundation for the growth of really large populations which are in turn essential for the development of complex cultures and social systems in a new "tribal" form of social organization. Land ownership became closely related to kin groups of clans and lineages, which were in turn the basis of formal systems of political authority based on elders or chiefs who could mediate in disputes and sometimes assume priestly functions. A whole variety of groups sprang up based not only on kinship but on residence, work, voluntary association, age, and gender and these group structures and hierarchical organization made it much easier to co-ordinate the larger populations that developed (see Hallpike 2008: 66-121). This tribal organization was the essential precursor of the state, particularly through the development of political authority which was always legitimated by descent and religious status. By the state I mean centralised political authority, usually a king, supported by tribute and taxes, and with a monopoly of armed force. Although it has been estimated that only about 20% of tribal societies in Africa, the Americas, Polynesia, New Guinea, and many parts of Asia actually developed the state, the state was almost as important a revolution in human history as agriculture itself, because of all the further developments it made possible, and a large literature on the process of state formation has developed (e.g., Claessen & Skalnik 1978, Hallpike 1986, 2008, Trigger 2003).

Unfortunately, Harari not only knows very little about tribal societies but seems to have read almost nothing on the literature on state formation either, which he tries to explain as follows:

> *The stress of farming [worrying about the weather, drought, floods, bandits, next year's famine and so on] had far reaching consequences. It was* the foundation *[my emphasis] of large-scale political and social systems. Sadly, the diligent peasants almost never achieved the future economic security they so craved through their hard work in the present. Everywhere, rulers and elites sprang up, living off the peasants' surplus food. (114)*

The reader might well wonder how peasants worrying about next year's possible famine could possibly have been the foundation of any major political developments, and why in any case they would have meekly allowed their crops to be plundered, as well as where these rulers and elites suddenly sprang from. If Harari knew more about tribal societies he would have realised that the notion of a leader imposing his will on his followers misses the whole point of leadership in pre-state societies, which is that the leader has to *attract* people by having something to offer them, not by threatening them, because he has no means of doing this. To have power over people one must control something they want: food, land, personal security, status, wealth, the favour of the gods, knowledge, and so on. In other words, there must be *dependency*, and leaders must be seen as benefactors. In tribal societies, where people are not self-sufficient in defence, or in access to resources or to the supernatural, they will therefore be willing to accept inequality of power because they obviously get something out of war-leaders, or clan heads, or priests. Political authority in tribal society develops in particular through the kinship system, with hereditary clan heads, who are also believed to have the mystical power to bless their

dependents. When states develop we always find that the legitimacy of
kings is based on two factors: descent and religion. It is only after the
advent of the state can power be riveted on to people by force whether
they like it or not, and when it is too late for them to do anything
about it except by violent rebellion.

Anyway, what was needed here to control these much larger populations were networks of mass co-operation, under the control of kings,
and Harari takes us almost immediately into the world of the ancient
empires of Egypt, and Mesopotamia, and Persia and China. But how
were these networks of mass communication created?

He recognises, quite rightly, the importance of writing and mathematics in human history, and claims they were crucial in the emergence
of the state:

> [I]n order to maintain a large kingdom, mathematical data was vital.
> It was never enough to legislate laws and tell stories about guardian
> gods. One also had to collect taxes. In order to tax hundreds of
> thousands of people, it was imperative to collect data about people's
> incomes and possessions; data about payments made; data about
> arrears, debts and fines; data about discounts and exemptions. This
> added up to millions of data bits, which had to be stored and processed.
> (137)

This was beyond the power of the human brain, however:

> This mental limitation severely constrained the size and complexity
> of human collectives. When the amount of people in a particular
> society crossed a critical threshold, it became necessary to store and
> process large amounts of mathematical data. Since the human brain
> could not do it, the system collapsed. For thousands of years after the
> Agricultural Revolution, human social networks remained relatively
> small and simple. (137)

But it is simply not true that kingdoms need to collect vast quantities
of financial data in order to tax their subjects, or that social systems

beyond a certain size collapsed until they had invented writing and a numerical system for recording this data. If Harari were right it would not have been possible for any kingdoms at all to have developed in Sub-Saharan Africa, for example, because there were no forms of writing systems in this region until quite late when a few developed under European or Islamic influence. (Ethiopia was a special case.) Nevertheless, pre-colonial Africa was actually littered with states and even empires that functioned perfectly well without writing.

They were able to do this because of the undemanding administrative conditions of early kingdoms. These are based on subsistence agriculture without money and have primitive modes of transport, unless they have easy access to river transport like Egypt, Mesopotamia or China. They also have a simple administrative structure based on a hierarchy of local chiefs or officials who play a prominent part in the organization of tribute. The actual expenses of government, apart from the royal court, are therefore relatively small, and the king may have large herds of cattle or other stock, and large estates and labourers to work them to provide food and beer for guests. The primary duty of a ruler is generosity to his nobles and guests, and to his subjects in distress, not to construct vast public works like pyramids. The basic needs of a ruler, besides food supplies, would be prestige articles as gifts of honour, craft products, livestock, and above all men as soldiers and labourers. In Baganda, one of the largest African states, with a population of around two million, tax messengers were sent out when palace resources were running low:

The goods collected were of various kinds—livestock, cowry shells, iron hoe-blades, and the cloths made from the bark of a fig-tree beaten out thin [for clothing and bedding]...Cattle were required of superior chiefs, goats and hoes of lesser ones, and the peasants contributed the cowry shells and barkcloths.... The tax-gatherers did not take a proportion of every herd but required a fixed number of cattle from each chief. Of course the hoes and barkcloths had to be new, and they were not made and stored up in anticipation of the tax-collection. It took some little time to produce the required number, and the tax-gatherers had to wait for this and then supervise the transport of the goods and cattle, first to the saza [district] headquarters and then to the capital. The amount due was calculated in consultation with the subordinates of the saza chiefs who were supposed to know the exact number of men under their authority, and they were responsible for seeing that it was delivered (Mair 1962: 163). (Manpower was recruited in basically the same way, and in Africa generally was made up of slaves and corvée labour.)

Nor do early states require written law codes in the style of Hamurabi, and most cases can be settled orally by traditional local courts. No doubt, the demands of administering early states made writing and mathematical notation very useful, and eventually indispensable, but the kinds of financial data that Harari deems essential for a tax system could only have been available in very advanced societies. As we have just seen, very much simpler systems were quite viable. (Since the Sumerian system of mathematical notation is the example that Harari chooses to illustrate the link between taxation, writing, and mathematics, it is a pity that he gets it wrong. The Sumerians did not, as he supposes, use a "a combination of base 6 and base 10 numeral systems". As is well-known, they actually used base 60, with sub-base 10 to count from 1–59, 61–119, and so on. [Chrisomalis 2010: 241-45])

When the Agricultural Revolution opened opportunities for the creation of crowded cities and mighty empires, people invented stories about great gods, motherlands and joint-stock companies to provide the needed social links. (115)

The idea of people "inventing" religious beliefs to "provide the needed social links" comes out of the same rationalist stable as the claim that kings invented religious beliefs to justify their oppression of their subjects and that capitalists did the same to justify their exploitation of their workers. Religious belief simply doesn't work like that. It is true, however, that what he calls universal and missionary religions started appearing in the first millennium BC.

> *Their emergence was one of the most important revolutions in history, and made a vital contribution to the unification of humankind, much like the emergence of universal empires and universal money.* (235)

But his chapter on the rise of the universal religions is extremely weak, and his explanation of monotheism, for example, goes as follows:

> *With time some followers of polytheist gods became so fond of their particular patron that they drifted away from the basic polytheist insight. They began to believe that their god was the only god, and that He was in fact the supreme power of the universe. Yet at the same time they continued to view Him as possessing interests and biases, and believed that they could strike deals with Him. Thus were born monotheist religions, whose followers beseech the supreme power of the universe to help them recover from illness, win the lottery and gain victory in war.* (242)

This is amateurish speculation, and Harari does not even seem to have heard of the Axial Age. This is the term applied by historians to the period of social turmoil that occurred during the first millennium BC across Eurasia, of political instability, warfare, increased commerce and the appearance of coinage, and urbanization, that in various ways eroded traditional social values and social bonds. The search for meaning led to a new breed of thinkers, prophets and philosophers who searched for a more transcendent and universal authority on how we should live and gain tranquility of mind, that went beyond the limits of their own society and traditions, and beyond purely material prosperity. People developed a much more articulate awareness of the mind and the self than hitherto, and also rejected the old pagan values of worldly success and materialism. As one authority has put it: "Everywhere one notices attempts to introduce greater purity, greater justice, greater perfection, and a more universal explanation of things" (Momigliano 1975: 8-9; see also Hallpike 2008: 236-65).

One of the consequences of this new cultural order was a fundamental rethinking of religion, so that the old pagan gods began to seem morally and intellectually contemptible. Instead of this naively human image of the gods, said the Greek Xenophanes, "One God there is ... in no way like mortal creatures either in bodily form or in the thought of his mind.... [E]ffectively, he wields all things by the thought of his mind." So we find all across the Old World the idea developing of a rational cosmic order, a divine universal law, known to the Greeks as Logos, to the Indians as Brahman, to the Jews as Hokhma, and to the Chinese as Tao. This also involved the very important idea that the essential and distinctive mental element in man is akin to the creative and ordering element in the cosmos, of Man as microcosm in relation to the macrocosm.

Intellectually, the idea that the universe makes sense at some deep level, that it is governed by a unified body of rational laws given by a divine Creator, became an essential belief for the development of science, not only among the Greeks, but in the Middle Ages and the Renaissance. As Joseph Needham has said, "...historically the question remains whether natural science could ever have reached its present stage of development without passing through a 'theological stage' " (Needham 1956: 582).

Against this new intellectual background it also became much easier to think of Man not as a citizen of a particular state, but in universal terms as a moral being. There is the growth of the idea of a common humanity which transcends the boundaries of nation and culture and social distinctions of rank, such as slavery, so that all good men are brothers, and the ideal condition of Man would be universal peace (Hallpike 2016: 167-218).

Harari tries to create a distinction between "monotheistic" religions such as Judaism, Christianity, and Islam, and "natural law religions", without gods in which he includes Buddhism, Taoism, Confucianism, Stoicism, and the Epicureans. From what I have said about the concepts of Logos, Hokhma, Brahman, and Tao it should be clear that his two types of religion actually had much in common. In Christianity, for example, Jesus was almost immediately identified with the Logos. The Epicureans, however, do not belong in this group at all as they were ancient materialist atheists who did not believe in natural law of any kind. One of the most obvious facts about states in history is that they all were hierarchical, dividing people into different classes with kings and nobles at the top enjoying wealth and luxury, and peasants or slaves at the bottom in poverty, men privileged over women, some ethnic groups privileged over others, and so on. Harari attributes all this to the invention of writing, and to the "imagined orders" that sustained the large networks involved in state organization:

> *The imagined orders sustaining these networks were neither neutral nor fair. They divided people into make-believe groups, arranged in a hierarchy. The upper levels enjoyed privileges and power, while the lower ones suffered from discrimination. Hammurabi's Code, for example established a pecking order of superiors, commoners and slaves. Superiors got all the good things in life. Commoners got what was left. Slaves got a beating if they complained.* (149)

But since these sorts of hierarchies in state societies are universal in what sense can they have simply been "make-believe"? Doesn't this universality suggest that there were actually laws of social and economic development at work here which require sociological analysis? Simply saying that "there is no justice in history" is hardly good enough. In particular, he fails to notice two very significant types of inequality, that of merchants in relation to the upper classes, and of craftsmen in relation to scholars, which had major implications for the development of civilisation, but to which I shall return later.

Harari says that religion and empires have been two of the three great unifiers of the human race, along with money: "Empires were one of the main reasons for the drastic reduction in human diversity. The imperial steamroller gradually obliterated the unique characteristics of numerous peoples ... forging out of them new and much larger groups" (213). These claims have a good deal of truth but they are also quite familiar, so I shall not go into Harari's discussion of this theme, except for his strange notion of "Afro-Asia", which he describes not only as an ecological system but also as having some sort of cultural unity, e.g. "During the first millennium BC, religions of an altogether new kind began to spread through Afro-Asia" (249). Culturally, however, sub-Saharan Africa was entirely cut off from developments in Europe and Asia until Islamic influence began spreading into West Africa in the eighth century AD, and has been largely irrelevant to world history except as a source of slaves and raw materials. And as Diamond pointed out in *Guns, Germs and Steel*, Africa is an entirely distinct ecological system because it is oriented north/south, so that it is divided by its climatic zones, whereas Eurasia is oriented east/west, so that the same climatic zones extend all across it, and wheat and horses for example are found all the way from Ireland to Japan.

Harari says that at the beginning of the sixteenth century, 90% of humans still lived in "the single mega-world of Afro-Asia", while the rest lived in the Meso-American, Andean, and Oceanic worlds. "Over the next 300 years the Afro-Asian giant swallowed up all the other worlds", by which he actually means the expanding colonial empires of the Spanish, Portuguese, Dutch, French and British. But to refer to these nations as "Afro-Asian" is conspicuously absurd, and the whole concept of Afro-Asia is actually meaningless from every point of view. The general idea of *Eurasia*, however, does make a good deal of cultural as well as ecological sense, not only because it recognises the obvious importance of Europe, but because of the cultural links that went to and fro across it, so that the early navigators of the fifteenth century were using the Chinese inventions of magnetic compasses, stern-post rudders, paper for their charts, and gunpowder, and were making their voyages to find sea-routes from Europe to China and the East Indies rather than relying on overland trade.

Harari's next major turning point in world history he refers to, reasonably enough, as "The Scientific Revolution". Around AD 1500 "It began in western Europe, a large peninsula on the western tip of Afro-Asia, which up till then played no important role in history" (272). This is a unconvincing assessment of a region that had been the seat of the Roman Empire, the Christian Church, and Greek science which was one of the essential foundations of the Scientific Revolution. Harari's opinions about how this got started are even less persuasive:

> *The Scientific Revolution has not been a revolution of knowledge. It has above all been a revolution of ignorance. The great discovery that launched the Scientific Revolution was the discovery that humans do not know the answers to their most important question. (279)*

This is a statement whose truth is not immediately obvious, and he justifies it as follows:

> *Premodern traditions of knowledge such as Islam, Christianity, Buddhism and Confucianism asserted that everything that is important to know about the world was already known. The great gods, or the one almighty God, or the wise people of the past possessed all-encompassing wisdom, which they revealed to us in scriptures and oral traditions. (279-80)*

These traditions may have claimed to know all that was essential to salvation and peace of mind, but that kind of knowledge had nothing whatsoever to do with pre-modern traditions of *science*. In Europe this meant Aristotle and Greek natural philosophy but about which, astonishingly, Harari has nothing at all to say anywhere in his book. Apart from a willingness to admit ignorance and embrace new knowledge, science:

...has a common core of research methods, which are all based on collecting empirical observations—those we can observe with at least one of our senses—and putting them together with the help of mathematical tools. (283)

This is a nineteenth-century view of what science does, whereas the really distinctive feature of modern science is that it tests theory by *experiment*, and does *not* simply collect empirical observations. On why modern science developed specifically in Europe Harari has the following explanation:

The key factor was that the plant-seeking botanist and the colony-seeking naval officer shared a similar mindset. Both scientist and conqueror began by admitting ignorance—they both said "I don't know what's out there." They both felt compelled to go out and make new discoveries. And they both hoped that the new knowledge would make them masters of the world. (316-17)

Botany was actually of quite minor importance in the early stages of modern science, which was dominated by studies of terrestrial and celestial motion (Copernicus, Galileo, Kepler, and Newton), and by chemistry which involved the revival of Greek atomism. And Columbus, to take a useful example of "a colony-seeking naval officer", knew quite well what was out there. He knew that the earth is round, and concluded that if he sailed west for long enough he would find a new route to the East Indies. So when he reached the islands of the Caribbean he was convinced that their inhabitants were "Indians" and never changed his mind. I think we can perhaps do a little better than Harari in explaining the European origin of modern science.

Greek science was dominated by the belief that reason, and particularly mathematics, was the true path to knowledge and its role was to be the tutor of the senses, not to be taught by them. The idea of performing an experiment did not really exist, and the great Alexandrian engineer Hero, for example believed that water pressure does not increase with depth. He defended this belief with an ingenious theory from Archimedes, but ignored the practical experiment of taking a glass down to the bottom of a pool where it could easily have been seen that the water rises higher inside the glass the deeper it is taken. Aristotle's theories of terrestrial and celestial motion, and Ptolemy's elaborate geometrical model of the heavens, for example, were seen as triumphs of reason, and were inherited by the medieval European universities who began a critical study of them. The importance of Greek science, however, was not that it was right—it contained fundamental errors—but that it presented a coherent theoretical model of how the world worked that stimulated thought and could be tested.

The Islamic world had transmitted much of Greek science to medieval Europe, and Aristotle in particular was greatly admired by Muslim scholars as "The Philosopher". But under the influence of the clerics Islam eventually turned against reason and science as dangerous to religion, and this renaissance died out. In rather similar fashion, the Byzantine Emperor Justinian closed the philosophy schools of Athens in 529 AD because he considered them dangerous to Christianity. But while in the thirteenth century several Popes, for the same reason, tried to forbid the study of Aristotle in the universities, they were ignored and in fact by the end of the century Aquinas had been able to publish his synthesis of Aristotelian philosophy and Christian theology in the *Summa Theologica*.

This illustrates a vital difference between Europe and the other imperial civilisations. Whereas the Caliph and the Byzantine Emperor had the authority to impose intellectual orthodoxy, in Europe the Popes could not enforce their will on society, and neither could the secular authorities, because there were too many competing jurisdictions—of the Holy Roman Emperor, of kings, of free cities, of universities, and between church and state themselves. Another vital difference was that in the other imperial civilisations there was that basic gulf between scholars and artisans and between merchants and the rest of the upper classes to which I referred earlier. Medieval European towns and cities, however, were run by merchants, together with the artisans and their guilds, so that the social status of artisans in particular was very much higher than in other cultures, and it was possible for them to interact socially with learned scholars. This interaction with scholars occurred in the context of a wide range of interests that combined book-learning with practical skills: alchemy, astrology, medicine, painting, printing, clock-making, the magnetic compass, gunpowder and gunnery, lens-grinding for spectacles, and so on. These skills were also intimately involved in the making of money in a commercially dynamic society.

It is highly significant that this interaction between scholars and artisans also occurred in the intellectual atmosphere of "natural magic", the belief that the entire universe is a vast system of interrelated correspondences, a hierarchy in which everything acts upon everything else. Alchemy and astrology were the most important components of this tradition, but by the thirteenth century Roger Bacon, for example, was arguing that by applying philosophy and mathematics to the study of nature it would be possible to produce all sorts of technological marvels such as horseless vehicles, flying machines, and glasses for seeing great distances. It was not therefore the admission of ignorance that was truly revolutionary, but the idea that science could be *useful* in mastering nature for the benefit of Man.

By the time of Galileo, whom Harari does not even mention, the idea that science should be useful had become a dominant idea of Western science. Galileo was very much in the natural magic tradition and was a prime example of a man of learning who was equally at home in the workshop as in the library—as is well-known, when he heard of the Dutch invention of the telescope he constructed one himself and ground his own lenses to do so. But Galileo was also enormously important in showing the crucial part that experiment had in the advancement of science. He was keenly interested in Aristotle's theory of terrestrial motion and is said to have tested the theory that heavier bodies fall faster than light ones by dropping them from the leaning tower of Pisa. This is somewhat mythical, but he certainly carried out detailed experiments with metal balls by rolling them down sloping planks to discover the basic laws of acceleration. He did not simply observe, but designed specific experiments to test theories. This is the hallmark of modern science, and it emerged in the circumstances that I have just described so that reason and the evidence of the senses were thus harmonized in the modern form of natural science. (On the origins of science see Hallpike 2008: 288-353; 396-428.)

Science, then, is not exactly Harari's strong point, so we need spend little time on the concluding part of his book, which is taken up with speculation about where science and technology are likely to take the human race in the next hundred years. He concludes, however, with some plaintive remarks about our inability to plan our future: "we remain unsure of our goals", "nobody knows where we are going", "we are more powerful than ever before, but have very little idea what to do with all that power" (465-66). He has just written a book showing that mankind's social and cultural evolution has been a process over which no-one could have had any control. So why does he suddenly seize upon the extraordinary fiction that there ought to be some "we" who could now decide where we all go next? Even if such a "we" existed, let us say in the form of the United Nations (!), how could it know what to do anyway?

Throughout the book there is also a strange vacillation between hard-nosed Darwinism and egalitarian sentiment. On one hand Harari quite justifiably mocks the humanists' naive belief in human rights, for not realising that these rights are based on Christianity, and that a huge gulf has actually opened up between the findings of science and modern liberal ideals. But on the other hand it is rather bewildering to find him also indulging in long poetic laments about the thousands of years of injustice, inequality and suffering imposed on the masses by the great states and empires of history, and our cruelty to our animal "slaves" whom we have slaughtered and exterminated in such vast numbers, so that he concludes, "The Sapiens reign on earth has so far produced little that we can be proud of." But a consistent Darwinist should surely rejoice to see such a fine demonstration of the survival of the fittest, with other species either decimated or subjected to human rule, and the poor regularly ground under foot in the struggle for survival. Indeed, the future looks even better for Darwinism, with nation states themselves about to be submerged by a mono-cultural world order, in which we ourselves are destined to be replaced by a superhuman race of robots. It has been rightly said that:

> *Harari's view of culture and of ethical norms as fundamentally fictional makes impossible any coherent moral framework for thinking about and shaping our future. And it asks us to pretend that we are not what we know ourselves to be—thinking and feeling subjects, moral agents with free will, and social beings whose culture builds upon the facts of the physical world but is not limited to them. (Sexton 2015: 120)*

Summing up the book as a whole, one has often had to point out how surprisingly little he seems to have read on quite a number of essential topics. It would be fair to say that whenever his facts are broadly correct they are not new, and whenever he tries to strike out on his own he often gets things wrong, sometimes seriously. So we should not judge *Sapiens* as a serious contribution to knowledge but as "infotainment", a publishing event to titillate its readers by a wild intellectual ride across the landscape of history, dotted with sensational displays of speculation, and ending with blood-curdling predictions about human destiny. By these criteria it is a most successful book.

René Girard's world of fantasy

The celebrated René Girard (1923–2015) spent the formative years of his academic career in the study of literature and literary theory, and when he retired in 1995 was still Professor of French Language, Literature and Civilization at Stanford University (Townsley 2003: 1). His literary researches, into ancient Greek mythology and drama as well as French and other modern European literature, also stimulated him to become a "philosophical anthropologist". In this capacity he became famous for his theory that communal violence, or the fear of it, underlay all human culture, and that sacrificial scapegoating, as the antidote to this violence, was the basis of all primitive religion, myth, ritual, and taboos. Unlike Claude Lévi-Strauss, he had little influence on social anthropologists, but he was nevertheless a major academic figure, especially in literary theory and religious studies. Author of around thirty books, he received many honorary degrees, was elected to the Académie Française and made a Knight of the Légion d'Honneur, and was described by one colleague as "the new Darwin of the social sciences". We are not, therefore, dealing with an obscure crank but with an important contemporary thinker with impressive credentials.

The foundation of the vast theoretical edifice that he built is actually quite a simple theory about violence and social control in primitive societies, which is a standard topic familiar to all anthropologists who have done field-work in these societies. A close and detailed knowledge of ethnographic facts is essential to an assessment of Girard's work, and in this paper I shall therefore draw in particular on my own years of field-work in Papua New Guinea and Ethiopia.

1. Girard's general theory

He starts from the premise that all human behaviour is learned, and
is therefore based on imitation, "mimesis". Our desires, in particular,
are not autonomous but learned from other people, and this typically
leads to conflict. To take a simple example, a child notices an object
and starts to play with it, whereupon another child sees this and wants
to play with it as well. This personal imitation or "acquisitive mimesis"
tends to generate violence, because the model and the imitator both
want the same thing, and it is hard to restrain the urge to violence that
develops: "…it is more difficult to quell an impulse to violence than to
rouse it, especially within the normal framework of human behaviour."
(Girard 1977: 1-2) In this situation other individuals are impelled to
join in by the same process of mimesis, so this anger generated within
the group must be vigorously discharged in some other way, and here
the scapegoat enters the picture. "If acquisitive mimesis divides by
leading two or more individuals to converge on one and the same object
with a view to appropriating it, conflictual mimesis will inevitably unify
by leading two or more individuals to converge on one and the same
adversary that all wish to strike down." (Girard 1987: 26)

The group thus choose some arbitrary victim to vent their fury upon,
instead of each other, and such victims are typically marginalised outsiders like children, old people, the disabled, women, and in particular,
animals. This victim becomes regarded as the cause of all the group's
troubles; their collective rage is discharged upon the scapegoat in the
ritual of sacrifice, the fury of the community then seems almost "mag-
ically" to cease, and calm is restored. Once the victim is expelled from
the community, the myth develops that not only was the scapegoat
responsible for the group's violence, but that by dying it was also
their salvation, and therefore god-like. Rituals develop around this
mythology, and over time animals take the place of human sacrificial
victims. But for the mechanism to work at all, it is essential that the
community does not realise that the scapegoat is really quite arbitrarily

chosen and has no responsibility for the group's troubles. If ever they should come to realise this, the whole sacrificial ritual would collapse.

It is important to note that in Girard's view, the original act of sacrifice was a real event in human history. "Ritual violence is intended to reproduce an original act of violence. There is nothing mythic about this original violence, but its ritual imitation necessarily includes mythic elements" (1977: 281). Surprisingly, Girard evidently supposes that this initial act took place far back in prehistory before humans acquired language. The first scapegoating ritual, being pre-linguistic, was simply based on instinct, and since scapegoating is the substitution of one thing for another it is also the origin of language, since words themselves are also substitutes for things. Sacrifice and the prohibitions associated with it would have created communal peace for early hominid groups and a safe space for mothers and their babies in particular.

The victimising process was therefore the missing link between the animal and human worlds that explains the humanisation of primates, and hunting and the domestication of animals were also motivated by the need for a stock of sacrificial victims. Scapegoating and sacrifice are the basis of all ritual and archaic religion generally, and archaic religion is the basis of all political and cultural institutions. Girard claims that the victimisation process is the rational principle that explains the infinite diversity of culture, and compares it to the principle of natural selection, which cannot be proved experimentally but convinces us by its great explanatory power.

Girard's belief that scapegoating could have been the source of language because it involves the substitution of the arbitrarily chosen victim faces two major problems, the first of which is a simple matter of evidence, or rather the lack of it. We simply know nothing about the thought processes of early hominids such as *Homo erectus*. Nor can we imagine what the social relations of pre-linguistic *Homo sapiens* might have been either, and attempts to do so are pure speculation. Indeed, we actually have no direct evidence for when grammatical language emerged. By "grammatical" I mean, for example, predication—the ability to say that something or someone has certain qualities; distinguishing between acting on and being acted upon; questions; negation, and referring to past and future. This raises the second problem, which is that it is hard to see how any symbolic culture would be possible at all without language. This is because the relation between a symbol and what it stands for, while drawn from nature, is not a representation of it. For example, among the Konso of Ethiopia, white is an inauspicious colour, but without language how could a group of people decide that white rather than black or some other colour should be regarded as inauspicious? (Indeed, how could the very idea of "inauspicious" come to be understood by a group of people without language?) In fact, the Konso regard white as inauspicious because it is the colour of bone, of death, therefore, and also the colour of cotton, which ripens during the hottest and driest part of the year. Black, on the other hand, is the colour of the life-giving rain-clouds and is therefore auspicious. But these are simply one set of symbolic values and other cultures have chosen different ones. In short, Girard does not explain how symbolic culture could have existed in a pre-linguistic society.

My objection is supported by the fact that archaeological evidence about the origins of human culture shows that self-decoration with coloured ochre, and simple shell necklaces, only started occurring around 100,000 years ago, but even this is not symbolic behaviour. (What, for example, is the symbolic meaning of a woman's lipstick?— nothing whatever.) The first clear evidence for *symbolic* culture comes from Europe about 40,000 years ago with the discovery of the Hohlenstein Lion Man (Cook 2013: 28-35). This is a statue carved from mammoth tusk which is a composite image with both human and leonine features; nothing like this exists in nature, of course, so there must have been some special conceptual association between humans and lions in that culture, and how could this association have been conveyed within the community except by language? The person who carved it must therefore have lived in a linguistic culture so that the statue could be given a meaning, even if this was as simple as "This is Ug, our lion god". Indeed, many scholars consider that it was in this period that fully grammatical language finally developed. Ritual, too, because of its many symbolic elements, can only inhabit a linguistic culture and cannot be derived from instinct as Girard attempts to do.

We can now move on to his general theory of imitation or mimesis. There is no doubt that human culture could not exist without imitation, notably by children imitating their parents and other adults. We all have a natural tendency to imitate our peers as well, and important people or classes also have a very powerful influence on fashions of all kinds. The overall effect of imitation is therefore to create social solidarity so it seems very strange, even perverse, that Girard considers it the principal basis of conflict. A fundamental weakness in his theory is that he assumes as the typical example of mimesis that only *one* object is available to be desired by the model, so that he and the imitator then inevitably come into competition over it, like the two children in the earlier example. But in fact this must be very rare, and what is far more typical is imitation of something that is readily reproduced and plentiful, such as a form of dress like a New Guinea penis-sheath, or some form of bodily decoration. We may imagine a prominent hunter who puts a streak of red ochre down his nose which is then imitated by all the other hunters in the band. Since there is plenty of red ochre to go around, how could this act of mimesis possibly bring about conflict? The obvious outcome is far more likely to be solidarity—the group now has its own emblem to distinguish itself from others.

This example also reminds us that imitation by itself is quite unable to explain culture, because someone has first to create or discover the desirable things that are imitated. The hunter who first put the red stripe down his nose, the child who first noticed the interesting toy, and the man who carved the Lion Man statue were all creators, not imitators. Societies, too, potentially have a wide range of traits which can be imitated, and this means that people must *choose* in some way

between these possibilities. Here again, mimesis is not enough to
explain the facts.

It has also been pointed out that as well as the "acquisitive mimesis"
that principally concerns Girard, there is also what can be called "beneficial mimesis", as when individuals provide models of good behaviour,
such as settling disputes, kindness, and generosity. But if there is such
a thing as beneficial mimesis this means that social peace can be re-
established by other means than scapegoating and sacrifice, as we know
from the many ceremonial forms of peace-making in primitive society.
(In fact, the more alternative forms of peace-making we can find, the
weaker Girard's whole theory becomes.)

2. Violence and sacrifice among the Tauade of Papua New Guinea

We can now consider the next part of Girard's theory, which is his
claim that acquisitive mimesis is actually the basic cause of violence
in primitive society. The Tauade of Papua New Guinea, with whom
I lived for a couple of years (Hallpike 1977), used to be one of the
most violent societies on record, so the ample data which we have on
this should provide us with an excellent test of Girard's hypothesis.
We find, however, that acquisitive mimesis has nothing whatever to
do with violence in their society, which is most typically provoked
by insult or other behaviour thought to show disrespect, theft of pigs
or other property, quarrels caused by pigs destroying gardens, or by
the sexual promiscuity of women. Violence from these quarrels is
then exacerbated by vengeance from the relatives and friends of those
involved. People feel that acting according to their feelings of the
moment is quite normal and appropriate, and impulsiveness is natural
for them. The following scene of village life taken from local court
records is a good example of what I have in mind:

*A man called Borowai Kowe described in court how "At Kavinivi one
day my uncle Avui Avila wanted to kill a pig so that he could buy a*

cross at the Mission store. So he asked his wife Kite to round up a pig but she refused [probably because she was angry about killing a pig for such a trivial reason]. Avui was cross, so he took some money and went down to another woman, also called Kite, and asked her for sex. She called out to her husband, Inawai, "Come quickly, Avui wants to have sex with me, make him give us a pig [in compensation for the insult]." Inawai called back, "It's only talk. He hasn't done anything, so let it go." Avui then went back to his own house, and after a row with his wife hit her on the back of the neck with the flat of his axe, and she fell down unconscious. Liam the Councillor, Sipitai, and Kinau ran past my house towards Avui's, all carrying axes, to help his wife Kite. [They were all her relatives.] Shortly afterwards I heard Avui call out, "They have killed me", [he had been axed in the chest by Liam the Councillor]. I went inside and got my bow and knife-bladed arrow and ran up towards Avui's house. [He was the narrator's uncle, remember.] There I saw Avui lying on his back on the ground, and his feet were kicking wildly. Around him were Liam, and two other men. Liam saw me and came towards me; as he stepped over the fence I shot him with my knife-bladed arrow in the stomach, and he stumbled forward and hit me with his axe on the arm. I ran on, and later I heard that my relative, the boy Kuruvu, had also been killed, as well as Liam and Avui."

According to Girard the Tauade and other societies in this situation of extraordinary community violence should have controlled it by the sacrifice of an animal or human scapegoat, which he assumes is the only mechanism available for defusing social conflict in primitive society. Now it is perfectly true that nothing unifies a group more effectively than a threat, particularly an enemy. This may be external, but an internal enemy, a traitor, a trouble-maker, a deviant, will do as well, and the group feels better if it has someone to bully and despise. But while every group and society contains despised groups and individuals, they are not normally killed or even necessarily ill-treated, let alone selected for slaughter. Not surprisingly, it is very hard to find eyewitness accounts of human sacrifice, but the following example is nevertheless very instructive. On Tonga in the early nineteenth century it is described (Martin 1827(I): 189-91) how in the course of warfare a warrior killed a man within a sacred enclosure, which was a very serious act of sacrilege. The priest of the temple was consulted, and revealed that a child must be sacrificed to appease the anger of the god, and the victim had to be a child of a chief by one of his concubines. The chiefs met to decide which of their number must provide the sacrifice, and one of the chiefs present agreed to allow his child, a little boy of two, to be the victim. He was then ritually strangled, and his body carried round all the neighbouring temples to appease their gods as well, before it was released to be buried. This sacrifice had nothing to do with restraining the warfare itself, which continued unabated, and the general emotion among the people involved was acute fear of the anger of the gods, not the rage of communal violence. The only other sentiment recorded was sadness for the little child—"Why are the gods so cruel?". Nothing here provides any support for Girard's theory of the human scapegoating sacrifice restoring community harmony. Among hunter-gatherers there are cases of notorious witches, or violent homicidal troublemakers who are collectively put to death by the rest of the band, with the consent of the victim's kin, but this, too, is rare and in any case is a perfectly rational procedure by people in fear of their lives.

So, returning to the Tauade, how then did they restrain communal violence? They had no class of elders, of respected senior men who could mediate in disputes, and while Big Men could control who used clan land, they, too, did not act as mediators in disputes. One method of controlling the spread of violence was avoidance, when a man who had killed someone would go and live elsewhere with his relatives in another group until tempers had cooled. The other principal method was compensation paid in pigs, dogs' teeth, or shells for homicide in particular, and for other offences like insults or property theft or damage. But where two groups had been fighting a communal pig feast was part of the procedure for re-establishing peaceful relations.

But, Girard might say, it is well-known that pig-killing is a central feature in traditional societies of Papua New Guinea, and the sacrificial relevance of this should be obvious. So let us see what light this throws on the significance of pig-killing among the Tauade as a means of restoring social harmony. In the first place, social harmony was never fully restored because people nursed grudges for generations and could suddenly take vengeance for killings that had happened many years previously. This is why the Tauade could not live in large villages but only in small hamlets. When asked why this was so, they would always reply, "Because of our fathers". They did have many ceremonial occasions when they killed pigs and distributed the meat, always accompanied by speeches. Traditionally it seems that the pigs were consecrated in a ritual manner when they were laid out for slaughter in the dance-yard, though this had lapsed by the time of my field-work. Girard would perhaps say that this was because the Australian Administration had imposed law and order. But it was still regarded as shameful to kill even a single pig without a formal distribution of meat and the giving of a speech and we may take this as a form of ritual consecration. For the Tauade, a great pig feast, accompanied by a dance and speeches, is *kova' karo namutu*, "really big power". *Kovata* has the meaning of physical energy, sorcery, and mystical power in general, and inheres in the blood in particular. It would be reasonable to think of the pig killings as releasing mystical power and so strengthening the community and its individual members. They will not kill their own pigs because, as they say, "they are like our own children", but they are quite willing to kill each other's and the pigs in the dance-yard are beaten to death with great ferocity, and traditionally were regarded as the enemy.

Major pig feasts of this kind were held at intervals of some years. They were not, however, responses to any crescendo of violence between local groups but rather to the size of the pig-herd that the prospective hosts had managed to build up. It is a matter of great prestige to be able to invite enemy groups in particular to such occasions, and the whole occasion is an opportunity for the hosts to humiliate their guests by their generosity, especially in the boastful speeches by the hosts' Big Men. The guests may have been sleeping in the dance village for weeks, being fed by their hosts, who are proud to see their own gardens devastated by the need to feed the visitors because it shows how generous they are and how productive their gardens are. The presentation of meat by the hosts after the pig killing is therefore ambivalent; in one respect it is a peace-offering, but the guests also feel humiliated by all this generosity, as they are intended to, and the hostility between guests and hosts, permanently simmering since they almost certainly have blood scores to settle, is given ritualised expression in the licence granted to guests to destroy pandanus and other trees, decorations, and gardens, and to fire arrows into or even destroy the men's house. In the past guests with their presents of pork might be sent on their way home with showers of arrows and abuse.

So while the ceremonial killing of pigs among the Tauade can be described as an example of sacrifice, in which the animals are treated as the enemy, it is essentially a competitive act that is simply one aspect of the eternally hostile relations between local groups. "Sacrifice" here is not a solution to communal violence in the sense of restoring amicable relations—indeed, the Tauade have no word for "peace"; it involves the slaughter of animals and not people but it is still a form of competition. There are also pig killings that are confined to the members of the local group, and their friends and relatives. Many of these are "rites of passage" held at significant points of individual life: birth, the initiation of boys, marriage, and death, or recovery from some injury or illness, or the return of a group member, and as such cannot in principle be responses to communal violence, any more than the large pig-killings are. The gifts of pork at such occasions are certainly intended as friendly acts to cement social relationships within the group and repay debts, but these occasions are also competitive displays intended to enhance the social status of those who provide the pigs. One of the marks of the "rubbish men" at the bottom of the social scale is that they are too pathetic to act as hosts on these occasions.

3. Violence and sacrifice among the Konso of Ethiopia

It is worth considering some comparative material from the Konso of Ethiopia here as a further test of Girard's general theory (Hallpike 2008). They have traditionally lived in large walled towns of some thousands of members in a complex and well-organised society that is very different from the Tauade. Battles between the towns frequently occurred in the traditional society before the Ethiopian government conquered the area. Occasions for these battles had nothing to do with acquisitive mimesis, however, and seem to have been acts of disrespect, such as trespassing on hunting territory, preventing people of another town using a path, throwing stones at their goats, and similarly trivial provocations. Within towns accusations of theft or of having the evil eye, drunkenness, or disputes over field boundaries were the sorts of thing that could lead to violence, but the whole ethos encouraged peace, social harmony, and good neighbourliness.

The Konso have a much more effective system of social control than the Tauade which, again, has nothing to do with scapegoating and sacrifice. First, everyone in a town is a member of a patrilineage whose head, the *poqalla*, can adjudicate disputes between its members, make land available to them, and is also a priest who sacrifices every year for the benefit of the lineage and its herds and crops. Each town is divided into wards with elected councils who can hear disputes between members of different lineages. Town members who misbehave can be publicly fined, and the disorderly arrested by the members of the warrior grade, and in the past serious thieves were executed. A man I knew who threatened to burn down his neighbour's house was expelled from the town altogether. A body of sacred office holders, the *Nama Dawra*, can also intervene if there are fights between the members of different wards and throw down their staves of office between the combatants. Bravery is highly admired, however, and men who had killed enemies in battle used to be commemorated by wooden mortuary statues, and age-sets whose warriors had killed enemies were also honoured by stone pillars in their name being erected in the public squares, or *moora*. On the other hand, they also think that warfare and the spilling of human blood pollutes the Earth, the source of life, so that in peace-making ceremonies after battles sacrifices were made to purify the Earth. But the towns are also organized into regions, at the head of which is a regional priest who was responsible for carrying out these sacrifices, and he also had his own *Nama Dawra* who would try to bring battles to an end by coming between the combatants and throwing down their staves.

Despite their various institutions for controlling violence, a number of ceremonies involving animal sacrifice are or were also performed. These were never a response to communal violence, but were dictated by the calendar or by some purely ritual necessity. The sacrificial animals are cattle, sheep, or goats, always male, and the victim is always consecrated before being killed, and the meat is always consumed by the "congregation". A few portions are reserved for certain categories of person, like the elders or the *Nama Dawra*, but unlike Papua New Guinea it is never given away as part of any system of gift exchange and hence this competitive element of Tauade feasts is absent. There is a basic belief that men's virility is threatened by sexually mature women or by bulls. So a bull that climbs onto the upper level of a homestead, the human level or *oita* forbidden to animals, is a threat to the virility of the head of the household, and has to be sacrificed. Similarly, a bull might climb on to the platform in the *moora* where the sacred emblems, the *ulahita*, of the warrior grade are standing. This platform is known as the *miskata*, and is forbidden to sexually mature women because they threaten the virility of the warrior grade. (It is thought that women make men soft, so that warriors should be unmarried.) So a bull that climbed onto the *miskata*, like the *oita*, has to be sacrificed. In a ceremony that I observed, after being consecrated the bullock was held up in the air by a group of young warriors, and one of them stabbed it in the chest with a spear. It was essential that it cried out when it was stabbed, and when it did so they all responded with a loud ceremonial shout, clearly signifying the conquest of an enemy. After this, the meat was eaten by those present. The same procedure was followed when an *ulahita* was erected and a he-goat was sacrificed. On the other hand, when a bullock was sacrificed for the annual feast of a working-party, or *marbara*, it was consecrated in the usual way, but its throat was simply cut and it died peacefully because the aim of the feast was to reinforce the comradeship of the *marbara* in a communal meal, and the bullock was not seen as a threat.

The other main type of sacrifice is performed at a certain time each year by the lineage head, the *poqalla*, for the health of the lineage members, their crops and animals. Here, a ram is the sacrificial animal; it is consecrated, then laid on its back on the ground, its mouth held tightly closed, and its throat cut. The meat is then eaten by all those present as an act of lineage harmony. It is said that it is a present to the Earth, just as the bullock held up and speared in the *moora* is a present to the Sky god. None of these sacrifices is engendered as the result of any social crisis of impending violence and disorder but are for religious purposes of one kind or another, and it is believed that social harmony itself produces harmony with nature. One can see no sign here either of acquisitive mimesis or scapegoating. The ram sacrificed by the *poqalla* is not treated as an enemy of any kind. The young bullock sacrificed in the *moora* is treated as a ceremonial enemy, but is not ill-treated beforehand, and is only an enemy in relation to the warrior grade.

Interestingly, there was a ritual process that can be considered as scapegoating and which is entirely different from the sacrifices I have been describing. In one of the regions, every ten years, a turtle used to be killed and its shell filled with earth from a dead man's grave, considered very impure. Turtles themselves are thought liable to be inhabited by well-spirits, because they are often found in wells and pools, but these spirits are not considered as real evil spirits though they can be dangerous. From my knowledge of Konso culture I think the killing of the turtle and the preparation of its shell would have been ritually consecrated. The shell with the earth was given to a man from outside Konso who was paid to travel slowly through the region for three months "to purify the land", as the people expressed it. He never entered any of the towns but lived in temporary shelters close by, and had food brought to him. It was very important that he should not be seen by women and children, and when he moved a horn was blown so that the women could hide. After three months, when he had visited all the towns of the region he took the shell with the earth in it down to the Sagan river, which forms one of the boundaries of Konsoland, and threw it in. He was not supposed ever to return to the region which was why he was an outsider. So while the Konso had the idea of casting all their sins on to some focus—the scapegoating of the turtle and the grave earth, which was then expelled—the effectiveness of the ritual depended on the three months of travel through the region, not from the sacrifice of the turtle alone.

There is, however, another ceremony in a different region where we can actually find evidence of human sacrifice. In order to understand what I am about to describe, it is necessary to realise first of all that for the Konso the hunting of dangerous animals like lions and leopards is a really important proof of manhood, like killing enemies in battle, and successful hunters have a triumph ceremony. Their society is also divided into "boys", unable to marry or have a triumph ceremony, "warriors", who may do both, and "elders", who act principally as councillors and mediators. But one is placed in the classes of boys, warriors, or elders not according to one's actual age, but by the position of one's *father* in the system. This means that there is not a close correlation between chronological and social ages, and many so-called "warriors" may in reality be young boys, for example. Promotion from one grade to the next only occurs every eighteen years, at a great ceremony, the Katapaha, which is held at this time for the promotion of the boys, Farayta, into the warrior grade, Xrela. One of the main features of this is the requirement of the Farayta boys to go into the bush and hunt for a dik-dik, or pygmy antelope, which they have to catch with their bare hands without shedding its blood, which of course is not real hunting at all, but play hunting. They bring it to the sacred place of the Moora Damalle to be sacrificed by the Bamalle, a regional priest, and its hide is cut into strips and distributed to the Farayta youths who are due to be promoted to Xrela.

What is the significance of the dik-dik here? As we have seen, the hunting of leopards and lions for the Konso is comparable to war, the fundamental test of manhood, and it is in this context that we have also to consider the sacrifice of the dik-dik here. The ritual status of the dik-dik is of particular interest because it is a very insignificant animal and is also wild, unlike cattle, sheep, and goats and in these respects quite different from the other examples of sacrificial animal. We can understand more about the dik-dik when we learn that it is a totem of Ishalayta clan, who are thought of as "innocent, kind-hearted, happy, harmless, and praiseworthy", and in the same way the dik-dik is a "harmless, grass-eating wild animal, known for its grace, calm, and peaceful life". In these respects it clearly has the innocent and harmless qualities of childhood, and I suggest that in fact it has to be understood as a symbol of childhood in Konso ritual.

This association with childhood becomes especially clear when we consider the details of a special hunting ceremony, the Karra, in which the men of one particular town go into the bush for several weeks to hunt a leopard and bring its skin back. The purpose of the ceremony, which is held in the tenth year after the Katapaha ceremony, is to mark the formal entry of the younger sons into Xrela, the warrior grade. At Katapaha only the eldest sons were formally inducted into Xrela, and their set was given its own name, but now it is the turn of their younger brothers also to formally become Xrela, and also be given their own set name. So in some ways it repeats the Katapaha ceremony in marking the induction of "boys" into warrior status, and here, too, the Karra ceremony also involves the hunt for the dik-dik and its sacrifice.

A little boy is recruited to act as the *inakarra*, "son of Karra", at least eight months before the beginning of the Karra. He is treated as a member of the senior set and therefore, despite his real age, as "old", and all ceremonial activities require his approval. He is groomed for the role by the *orkipa,* the leaders of the senior set, and fed with a special diet of meat, butter, and beer brewed with honey, all of these being the classic marks of consecrating a victim for sacrifice. He is also required to taste the food of every feasting group during the Karra before anyone else partakes of it. One of the *inakarra's* first duties is to lead a group of *orkipa* to the Bamalle's homestead where the Bamalle performs a ritual in which he symbolically sharpens a bunch of their spears. The *orkipa* present him with a gourd of milk from the first lactation of a cow, and another of grain. The Bamalle asperses the group and blesses them: "Let your spear be sharp; let it kill; have luck with your kill; Korria (Konso), I have blessed you; catch the game with bare hands; find it timid; get it without spears, without difficulty, without danger; be plenty; be strong". There are really two blessings here, one for the real hunters of leopards or lions, who will need sharp spears, but the second blessing with the reference to catching game with bare hands is not for the real hunters, however, but to the boys of the younger set who will hunt the dik-dik.

In the weeks before the hunt for a leopard begins the *inakarra* leads the boys, who will later form the new set, Karmoha, down to the lowlands where they are expected to catch a dik-dik with their bare hands, without harming it or shedding its blood, and take it back to the Bamalle. Remarkably, it appears that in the not very distant past (around 1950) the *inakarra* was in fact abandoned there to die[1], or at least to make his way home unaided. It was said that even if some *inakarra* survived, they became deaf and dumb or mentally retarded, and this therefore seems to have been a form of child sacrifice. (Indeed, it is possible that Katapaha itself also involved a similar child sacrifice, since at the time of the 1971 Katapaha the Governor of Konso had to promise the Provincial Governor that he would ensure that no such thing would occur.) What, then, is the significance of the child sacrifice here?

In the Karra ritual the dik-dik is brought back by the boys from the lowlands and then sacrificed by the Bamalle. Its skin is cut into strips on which are sewn nine cowries in three rows, that are worn on the little finger of the left hand (obviously the weakest of all the fingers) by a group of young boys, numbering about 12, known as the *chehiteta*. These are recruited from the teenagers who will shortly become the youngest age-set, Karmoha, of the warrior grade. They assemble in an abandoned residence of the town and who, as a rite of manhood, are made to copulate with a divorced lady who volunteers to do this. Those who *refuse to do this* (or are perhaps too young) are selected to be the *chehiteta* and wear the cowries (which are female symbols, it should be noted) on the dik-dik skin, in addition to carrying out errands from the hunting ground to the town every time they are requested to.

The dik-dik is therefore a central ritual element in both the Katapaha and the Karra, involving the attainment of warrior status by those hitherto classified as "boys", as children. The hunt for the dik-dik is not real hunting at all, but play hunting since it must be caught with bare hands and its blood must not be shed until it is sacrificed. The strips of its skin with feminine cowrie shells are carried on the weakest finger by those *chehiteta* who have not had intercourse with the *arapalayta*, and this suggests that it has a general association with weakness and general lack of manliness, quite the opposite of the bull or the leopard. I propose, therefore, that the poor little *inakarra* is to the adult hunters what the poor little dik-dik is to the leopard, and that the *inakarra* is therefore the symbol of childhood which, like the little boy himself, has to be ritually abandoned in the bush before real manhood can be attained.

4. Conclusions

Understanding sacrifice in any particular society is a complex matter, then, as these examples have shown, and requires detailed knowledge of the culture. Knowledge of Tauade culture shows us that sacrifice can have many different occasions and a number of different purposes: it serves to enhance community solidarity but only in competition with other groups, and individual reputation in competition with other members of the group. Pig killings are not scapegoating and not a response to communal violence, but are a form of social competition and the ceremonial marking of significant events and rites of passage in individual lives. Sacrifice among the Konso cannot generally be explained in terms of scapegoating either; there is a specific and unusual ritual for this in one region, but while the sacrificed bullock is treated as the enemy of the warrior grade it is not a scapegoat. The sacrifice of the ram by the *poqalla* for his lineage is quite different in nature, and we have seen that the significance of the *inakarra's* sacrifice lies in the symbolic opposition between childhood and manhood.

Again, the frenzied outbursts of communal violence which Girard sees as a permanent threat hanging over primitive societies in general also bear no relation to reality as far as people like the Konso are concerned, since they have a well-developed set of procedures and institutions for maintaining the peace and controlling violence that are also quite independent of sacrifice. Even in Papua New Guinea the violence of the Tauade comes nowhere close to consuming society. While they are much less able to control violence than the Konso are, compensation and avoidance are still reasonably effective in limiting its effects, and we have also seen that pig-killing ceremonies in general have no particular relation to communal violence.

At the end of this enquiry the facts therefore give considerable support to Hubert and Mauss who say that sacrifices have a great diversity of forms and purposes, and that it is quite false to suppose that "all the possible kinds of sacrifice have emerged from one primitive, single form" in the manner Girard proposes. (Hubert & Mauss 1964: 95) On the contrary, the only unity that the institution possesses is an abstract structure in which a victim is first sacralised or consecrated, and finally destroyed:

> *[F]undamentally, beneath the diverse forms it takes, it always consists in one procedure, which may be used for the most widely differing purposes. This procedure consists in establishing a means of communication between the sacred and profane worlds through the mediation of a victim, that is, of a thing that in the course of the ceremony is destroyed. (ibid., 97)*

Girard, however, dismisses Hubert and Mauss, but his alternative theory of the mimetic causation of violence, and of sacrifice as a scapegoating mechanism to restrain it, is contradicted by the facts on every hand, as we have seen from even the small sample presented here, and is wholly untenable from the anthropological point of view. The same can be said of his complete obsession with violence. This being so, his whole theoretical edifice is shown to be without foundation and simply collapses. While he quotes some very sound anthropologists like Evans-Pritchard, Lienhardt, Victor Turner, and Chagnon, he has no scholarly understanding of primitive society, which requires very much more intellectual background than pulling a few books off library shelves. It is a curious feature of the intellectual world that many people think themselves perfectly qualified to dogmatise about primitive society while knowing very little about it. Evolutionary psychologists are one example, and Girard is another. There are some theories in anthropology that many of us consider mistaken, like cultural materialism for example, but at least they are supported by evidence and rational arguments. One is unable to say the same of Girard's ideas, however, and it is quite remarkable that he could have spent so much time and effort writing so many books, and constructing this grandiose theory of "philosophical anthropology", this world of fantasy, without bothering to run it past a few real anthropologists who could have told him that he was certainly not "the new Darwin of the social sciences".

Notes

1. Because of the treatment of the child, there were apparently a number of court cases in about 1950, as a result of which the custom was abandoned, and now the *inakarra* is only symbolic, consisting of a *jika* spearhead wrapped in a cloth called *charfa* with an ostrich feather tied to its tip as though it were a human head (see Hallpike 2008: 322).

The Man-Eating Myth reconsidered

In this gallery of absurd theories about primitive Man I find serious fault with a variety of biologists, evolutionary psychologists, literary philosophers, linguists, historians and journalists, but in fairness a space should also be found for some anthropologists. Some time ago I dissected Professor Adam Kuper's claim that there is no such thing as primitive society (Hallpike 1992), but another prize candidate for the butcher's block has to be Professor William Arens's book *The Man-Eating Myth*. It was published by Oxford University Press in 1979, and claims that cannibalism is a racist and colonialist myth perpetuated by Westerners, including credulous anthropologists who should know better, and that there is no reliable eyewitness evidence that it ever existed as a social custom in any society (as distinct from occasional "survival cannibalism"). The book created something of a sensation when it appeared, and although we are approaching its fortieth anniversary it is still in print, with respectable sales on Amazon and discussed at great length in Wikipedia, and so seems worth a further assessment. Besides telling post-modernist academia what it wanted to hear, it has clearly satisfied a popular need as well, about which the following extract from a review on Amazon gives us a clue:

> *The reason this book caused such a ruckus when it was released, is not just the fact that it made anthropologists look as disreputable as phrenologists: charlatans, shysters and hucksters practicing a crank pseudoscience. Among the highly educated, it's fashionable to ridicule the bumpkins and yokels for being gullible enough to buy into astrology,*

creationism and other forms of nonsense. But as W. Arens proved with "The Man-Eating Myth", the intelligentsia is just as easily fooled as what Mencken called 'the booboisie'[1] and that in many cases, 'PhD' means 'piled high and deep'.

It is undoubtedly true that cannibalism is the feature of primitive society most apt to be sensationalised by the popular press in particular, and books with titles like *Where Cannibals Roam*, *A Naturalist in Cannibal Land*, *The Last Cannibals*, *Mountains, Gold and Cannibals*, or *Two Years Among New Guinea Cannibals* are sure to find eager readers. Anthropologists would also agree that many accounts of cannibalism are exaggerated, based on rumour, or simply false. Probably all societies have contrasting images of the wild and the tame or social: standard images of the wild are incest as opposed to respect for kinship rules, eating food raw as opposed to cooked, nudity as opposed to clothing, hairiness and long hair as opposed to smooth skin and short hair, and eating human flesh as opposed to animal flesh, so it is not surprising that accusations of cannibalism are often used to stigmatize "the other". For example, the Konso had a horror of cannibalism, and a very old man told me that in his youth he had been to Addis Ababa (about four hundred miles to the north) on an errand for the Imperial Government. He stayed there for some time, and on his way back he was misdirected about the road, and after walking "for a year" he reached the land of the cannibals, the *pulkoota*. Their mouths, he said, "stuck out like this"— holding his fingers towards his mouth and clearly indicating an ape-like face—and they had tails and eyes in the backs of their heads. They used to buy people and also kept prisoners captured in battle. They would cut them up into strips and hang these up to dry. They lived only on human flesh and cultivated no fields. He managed to avoid them and eventually made his way back to Konso (Hallpike 2008: 379). And when I first began living among them, some of the mothers would tell their children that if they did not be quiet and go to sleep the terrible white man would come and eat them. The Konso conception of cannibalism is an excellent example of a pervasive theme of Arens's book, that cannibalism is a stigmatization of the savage "other".

If this were all that Arens is saying it would be accepted as a commonplace of anthropology, but he raises the commonplace to the sensational by claiming that there is no evidence that cannibalism has ever existed at all: "[E]xcluding survival conditions, I have been unable to uncover adequate documentation of cannibalism as a custom in any form for any society. Rumors, suspicions, fears and accusations abound, but no satisfactory first-hand accounts." Although we may find this extremely surprising, he nevertheless goes on to assure us that "I have marshalled the available material to support this premise, rather than manipulating the data to generate the kind of foregone conclusion which characterizes the current thinking on this topic" (Arens 1979: 21-22).

Before we go any further, however, it is very striking that Arens never makes any attempt to explain why the *refusal* to eat human flesh must apparently be such a powerful and universal human imperative that cannibalism has never existed anywhere as an accepted social practice. He simply assumes it to be self-evident. One might be unwilling to believe, in principle, that any society could possibly have institutionalised incest between mothers and sons, or the eating of human faeces, for example. But in primitive societies especially, meat is highly prized, particularly by those dependent on agriculture because they can only eat it relatively seldom. Since people in many societies are willing to eat stinking meat, why is it inconceivable for them to eat fresh human meat, especially of enemies killed in battle? Indeed, the *idea* of cannibalism is quite familiar to Christians when they take the sacraments of Christ's Body and Blood. Arens's unwillingness to believe in the very possibility of cannibalism as an institution appears, in fact, to be his own ethnocentric Western prejudice.

His demand for eyewitness evidence begins with the undoubted fact that "cannibalism is an observable phenomenon" but proceeds to the very dubious inference that therefore "the evidence for its existence should be derived from observation by reliable sources" (21), meaning "those trained in the craft of ethnography". There are in fact plenty of eye-witness accounts of cannibalism: "Claims of having observed cannibalism first-hand are rampant in the travelogues of explorers, missionaries, explorers, sailors and their ilk" (35). But he dismisses all these as having "little if any credibility", and continues:

> *Leaving this brand of literature behind, and examining instead the production of professional anthropologists, the problems change but the situation still remains perplexing. From all corners of the globe the reports come in that a specific group of people has lived among were cannibals long ago, until pacification, just recently or only yesterday. The reader is engulfed by a stream of past tenses denoting varying removes in time, indicating a demise of custom some time before the researcher took up residence upon the scene. (35-6)*

With one trivial exception of the ritual consumption of human ashes, which he rejects, he claims that no modern anthropologist has witnessed the consumption of human flesh by the people he or she was studying. This is hardly surprising, of course, since colonial administrators and missionaries had suppressed cannibalism, so by the time the anthropologists came on the scene they were too late to observe it. But not only does Arens dismiss eyewitness accounts by those not "trained in the craft of ethnography", but is almost equally contemptuous about anthropologists generally and New Guineanists in particular, where apparently "academic standards seem to function as an almost forgotten ideal, rather than as standard operating procedure. Anthropologists with well-deserved reputations based upon previous research and publication become the victims of their own sensationalism and poor scholarship" (99).

The anthropologist Klaus-Friedrich Koch, for example, supplies copious details of cannibalism among the Jale of West New Guinea (Irian Jaya), such as:

Cannibalism is an integral part of a particular kind of war. The Jale
distinguish between a wim *war and a* soli *war. Only* soli *warfare*
ideally features anthropophagic revenge. While a wim *war always*
ends within a few years and may last only for a day or two, a soli
war usually endures for a much longer time and may extend over
the period of a generation.... Wim *warfare occurs between two or*
more wards of the same village, between two segments of the same
ward living temporarily at different localities such as garden hamlets,
or between two or more villages in the same district or adjacent
districts. Soli *wars, on the other hand, are usually waged between two*
villages separated by a wide river or by a mountain ridge, a geographic
condition that puts them in different districts or regions. Informants
repeatedly stated the maxim that "people whose face is known should
not be eaten". In practice immunity from anthropophagic vengeance
derives from the nature and relative frequency of affinal links between
two villages. (Koch 1974: 79-80)

Arens, however, simply dismisses all Koch's research as the result
of missionary propaganda, since he cannot claim to have witnessed
cannibalism himself (Arens 1979: 98) but fails to ask himself the next
and perfectly obvious question: "Where, then, did Koch get all this
stuff about cannibalism—did he just make it all up?" Obviously he
didn't, and got it from his informants as he makes abundantly clear in
his book, but it would be inconvenient for Arens to admit this since,
as we have noted, it is one of the themes of his book that accounts of
cannibalism are inherently hostile and derogatory lies told about *other*
peoples, and not about one's own.

Why, however, would the Jale say they had been cannibals if they
hadn't, and why did the Tauade happily admit to me that they had
been cannibals too, referring to enemy groups with a laugh as "our
meat, like pork". In my book *Bloodshed and Vengeance in the Papuan
Mountains* (1977) I give the following account of a cannibalistic event
told to me by my best informant, Amo Lume:

*While the initiation ceremony was in progress the Gane men made
an attack. The Goilala seized their weapons and chased the Gane.
There was a big battle. Aima Kamo speared Kog Kanumia Konoina,
and Aima Kovio also speared him, and Koupa Teva axed him, as
did Orou Keruvu, and Mo Kimani, chief of Watagoipa. Everyone
came and chopped him to pieces. The Tawuni and Kataipa,* valavala
*[allies] of the Goilala, were invited to take the bits home to eat. Kolalo
Kioketairi (who had a twisted lip because he had cut his mouth while
removing human flesh from a bone) cut off Kog Kanumia's head and
took it to Dimanibi singing a song. [Then the storyteller retraces his
steps to give some further details.]*

*[T]he Tawuni and Kataipa took away their pork [given by the
Goilala to celebrate the victory] with Kog Kanumia of Gane's body.
They dismembered Kog at the Kovelaiam bridge over the Kataipa
river, and made a big oven [an earth oven with hot stones], in which
they cooked the pork and Kog Kanumia at the same time. Kolalo tied
a vine to Kog Kanumia's head and held it over the fire to singe off the
hair [pigs similarly have their hair singed off before cooking], then
cooked it in the oven. When it was taken out, he skinned the face
and feasted on the white flesh beneath. After this the Tawuni and
Kataipa went back to their places. (Hallpike 1977: 213)*

The remark about "the white flesh" beneath the dark skin of the face
is interesting, because in fact even dark-skinned human flesh, when
cooked, does indeed turn white, like pork and chicken, a realistic
detail which gives additional credibility to the story. Arens dismisses
my account of Tauade cannibalism, carefully ignoring the episode just
described, but again fails to answer the basic question of why on earth
the Jale, the Tauade, and many other peoples of Papua New Guinea
would claim to have been cannibals themselves in the past if this were
not true.

In the same way as these accounts of cannibalism from native informants, anthropologists have had to rely on the people's recollection of

other aspects of their life and culture that were suppressed or had died out, like warfare or exposing corpses to rot, or initiation ceremonies, but should it be assumed that native informants were lying or mistaken about all these as well? It seems a curiously disrespectful attitude to indigenous peoples to dismiss all their recollections of their own past as unreliable. The Tauade used to be one of the most violent societies on record, and my informants gave me copious accounts of all manner of warfare and mayhem, which were supported by government records, but during the two years I lived with them I never witnessed a single homicide apart from an accident, or even a physical assault, let alone a battle, yet these are all highly observable phenomena nonetheless.

So the reason that so many anthropologists' accounts of societies in Papua New Guinea mention cannibalism is not because they had "become the victims of their own sensationalism and poor scholarship", but because their informants told them a great deal about it. By contrast, a survey of the historic literature and modern ethnography of the Cushitic-speaking peoples of the Horn of Africa, which include the Konso, reveals virtually nothing on the subject of cannibalism, except one or two vague references in the earlier literature. This is not because anthropologists working in this area were more objective than those working in New Guinea, but simply because there was probably little or no cannibalism in the Horn of Africa.

At this point it is time to revert to Arens's "basket of deplorables", all those travellers, missionaries, and old sea-faring men he so despises; according to Arens, "The legion of reports by non-specialists were found to range from highly suspect to entirely groundless when viewed from the perspective of objective scholarship and common sense" (181), whereas they actually provide some of the best material on cannibalism. Arens's complete denial of cannibalism puts him in the same logical position as someone who insists that all swans must to be white, and that accounts of black swans are absurd myths only believed by the ignorant and credulous: it simply takes one example of a black swan for the whole theory to start unravelling—if one, why not others? My black swan for Arens is the following eyewitness account of Maori cannibalism by Captain Cook. It can most easily be found in Beaglehole's standard and readily available biography of Cook (1974) by looking in the index under "Cook, James, reflections on cannibalism", which took me all of five minutes to unearth. Beaglehole takes the account from Cook's *Journal* for 23 November 1773 in Queen Charlotte Sound, New Zealand, and it reads as follows[2]:

There had been rumours of a war expedition to Admiralty Bay, lately picked human bones had been found, when on 23 November, with Cook anxious to get to sea but prevented by the wind, some of the officers went on shore to amuse themselves and were confronted by the remainders of a cannibal feast. The broken head and the bowels of the victim were lying on the ground, his heart was stuck on a forked stick fixed to the head of a canoe. Pickersgill gave two nails for the head and took it on board, to the interest of a number of New Zealanders on board who had not participated in the banquet. Would one of them like a piece? asked Clerke, "to which he very chearfully gave his assent"; Clerke cut a piece and broiled it in the galley, and the man devoured it ravenously. At that moment Cook, who had been absent, came on board with Wales, Forster, and the young islander Odiddy [not a Maori], to find the quarter-deck crowded and excitement general. Revolted as he was, the spirit of science triumphed, he must be able to bear witness from his own eyes to a fact that many people had doubted on the first voyage reports; Clerke broiled another piece, it was similarly consumed before the whole ship's company; some were sick; Odiddy, first motionless with horror, burst into tears and abused Clerke as well as the New Zealanders, up till then his friends; Wales and Cook thought it over. (Beaglehole 1974: 358-59)

Captain Cook is renowned as one of the most meticulous and objective of observers, and it did not take someone "trained in the craft of ethnography" to describe this particular incident. But if one finds a black swan it could hardly be the only one, and statistically one would expect that a number of others also existed. The most effective method of proving that something like cannibalism does *not* exist, would be to find cases where the evidence for it seemed to be the strongest, and then try to demonstrate that in fact this so-called evidence is fabricated or otherwise too weak to prove the case. If the strongest cases fail to demonstrate the existence of cannibalism, then it is a reasonable inference that weaker cases are likely to fail as well, even if we cannot examine all of them.

Anthropologists, among many others, have long considered that before colonial rule the Maori of New Zealand, many New Guineans, and the Fijians were cannibals, which is why I naturally went first to the records of Captain Cook. Arens, however, in "marshalling the available material", *does not mention the Maori at all*, about whom there is clear evidence of cannibalism from many sources (see Jennings 2004, for example), and in the index of his book the Fijians rate only one mention, p.176. Turning to this, and expecting at least some discussion of their celebrated cannibalism, one finds only a reference to a Hawaiian gift shop: "Here they can purchase 'Authentic Cannibal Forks' made in Fiji which, the package instructs the buyer, were originally used by the chiefs, since it was *tapu* for such food to touch their lips. It adds that missionaries stopped the practice, and suggests instead that the owner can now use these instruments as 'pickle forks'" (Arens, p.176). And this is all the evidence that Arens can marshal on the topic of Fiji, one of the most intensively studied examples of institutionalised cannibalism in the ethnographic literature.

There are many eyewitness accounts of Fijian cannibalism from the nineteenth century, of which one of the best known is that of William Endicott (1923) based on his experiences in March 1831, as third mate of the *Glide*.[3] He describes going on shore after hearing that the nearby village are celebrating the arrival of three enemy corpses, killed in a recent battle, and which had been brought back to be eaten (*bakola*). One of the bodies was given to a neighbouring village but the other two were prepared for the oven:

The heads of both savages being now taken off, they next cut off the right hand and the left foot, right elbow and left knee, and so in like manner until all the limbs separated from the body (see Sahlins 1983: 81-2 for confirmation of this ritual practice). [After a special piece was cut from the chest for the King] The entrails and vitals were then taken out and cleansed for cooking. But I shall not here particularise. The scene is too revolting. The flesh was then cut through the ribs to the spine of the back which was broken, thus the body was separated into two pieces. This was truly a sickening sight. I saw after they had cut through the ribs of the stoutest man, a savage jump upon the back, on end of which rested upon the ground, and the other was held in the hands and rested upon the knees of another savage, three times before he succeeded in breaking it. This ended the dissection of the bodies (Endicott 1923: 62). [A fire-pit had been dug about 6 feet in diameter and one and a half deep, and lined with stones, and a large fire made in it, into which small stones were placed.]

[A]s the bodies are cut to pieces they are thrown upon the fire, which after being thoroughly singed are scraped while hot by the savages, who sit around the fire for this purpose. The skin by this process is made perfectly white, this being the manner in which they dress their hogs, and other animal food. (ibid., 63)

The head of the savage which was last taken off, was thrown towards the fire, and being thrown some distance it rolled a few feet from the men who were employed around it; when it was stolen by one of the savages who carried it behind the tree where I was sitting. He took the head in his lap and after combing away the hair from the top of it with his fingers picked out the pieces of the scull which was broken by the war club and commenced eating the brains. This was too much for me. I moved my position, the thief was discovered and was as soon compelled to give up his booty, it being considered by the others he had got by far too great a share. The process of cleansing and preparing the flesh occupied about two hours. There was no part of these bodies which I did not see cleansed and put in the oven.

The stones which had been placed upon the fire were now removed, the oven cleaned out, the flesh carefully and very neatly wrapped in fresh plantain leaves and placed in it. The hot stones were also wrapped in leaves and placed among the flesh, and after it was all deposited in the oven, it was covered up two or three inches with the same kind of leaves, and the whole covered up with earth of sufficient depth to retain the heat. (ibid., 63-4)

This construction of the earth oven was exactly the same as that which I observed among the Tauade. It was not due to be opened until after midnight, so Endicott went off and did not return to the house where the feast was until shortly before dawn, when he found that the feast had been going on for some time. But he was not too late, and was offered a piece of meat: "It was accordingly brought carefully wrapped in a plantain leaf as it had been placed in the oven. I unwrapped it and found it to be a part of a foot taken off at the ankle and at the joints of the toes. I made an excuse for not eating it, by saying that it had been kept too long after it was killed, before it was cooked, it being about thirty-six hours" (ibid., 66-7). (Other seamen from the *Glide,* who also went ashore, independently confirmed the basics of Endicott's account, see Sahlins 2003: 5.)

Not everyone believed this and other accounts, and Sahlins comments:

Faced by a similar incredulity, another British captain, Erskine of HMS Havannah, *was compelled to preface his discussion of Fijian cannibalism by lengthy quotations from eyewitness reports of earlier European visitors. These include accounts from the voyage of the* Astrolabe *(1838), the US Exploring Expedition (1840), and from the missionary-ethnographer John Hunt (1840). Erskine also prints*

*in full the narrative of John Jackson, a seaman resident in Fiji from
1840 to 1842, which contains three detailed descriptions of cannibal
feasts (pp. 411-477). (Sahlins 1979)*

There are many other eye-witness accounts of Fijian cannibalism
from the nineteenth century, of which Sahlins mentions, in particular:

(1) Mary Wallis, the wife of a bêche-de-mer *trader, was in Fiji
for about 46 months between 1844 and 1851. Her diaries (1850;
1994) record some 32 cannibal events—I may be off by one or two—
in 21 different locations, many involving multiple* bakola. *There
are also five or six more general discussions of cannibal practice;
(2) Rev. Thomas Williams's published journal (1931) reports 28
cannibal incidents (including some in editorial notes, mainly from
Williams's other writings) at 17 locations, and also includes five general discussions (cf, Williams and Calvert 1859); (3) in Rev. Joseph
Waterhouse's book on Bau (1866) there are 24 instances at ten or
more places, plus ten general discussions. (Sahlins 2003: 5).*

Sahlins gives a general description of how cannibalistic symbolism
permeated the whole Fijian way of life. It was expressed in:

…the specific drumbeats announcing the taking of bakola *[cannibal
victims]; the pennants flying from the masts of victorious canoes
signifying* bakola *on board; the ovens reserved for cannibal feasts; the
special stones near the temple on which* bakola *were carved up; the
sacred trees on which their genitals were hung; the (natural) bamboo
splints used to carve human flesh and the elaborately fashioned forks
used to eat it; the distinctive dances, songs and unrestrained joy with
which young women, dressed in finery, greeted the return of successful
warriors; the sexual orgies while the bodies were cooking; the ritual
consecration of warriors who had killed and the enshrinement of
their war clubs in the temples; the miserable afterlife of unsuccessful
warriors, pounding a pile of shit through all eternity; the gourmet*

debates about body parts; the taboos on human flesh for certain persons; the cures effected by pressing cooked bakola *flesh to the lips of afflicted children; the sail needles made from the bones of notable* bakola *and the poetry from their fate. (Sahlins 2003: 4, and see also Sahlins 1983: 72-93)*

Not all cannibalism, by any means, was so bound up in the culture's religious and social life, and could be quite perfunctory. Mr William Mariner was a young captain's clerk who was captured by the Tongans in 1806 when they seized his ship and killed most of the crew. He became a favourite of King Finow, learnt the language, and was a close and very intelligent observer of Tongan life until he managed to escape in 1810. (On his return to London he was befriended by a physician, Dr John Martin, who published an account of his experiences.) During one of the many wars in which Mariner was involved he made the following observation on cannibalism:

The following day, some of the younger chiefs, who had contracted the Fiji habits *[my emphasis] proposed to kill the prisoners, lest they should make their escape, and then to roast and eat them. The proposal was readily agreed to, by some, because they liked this sort of diet, and by others because they wanted to try it, thinking it a manly and warlike habit. There was also another motive, viz. A great scarcity of provisions; for some canoes which had been sent to the Hapai islands for a supply were unaccountably detained, and the garrison was already threatened with distress. Some of the prisoners were soon despatched; their flesh was cut up into small portions, washed with sea-water, wrapped up in plantain leaves, and roasted under hot stones; two or three were embowelled, and baked whole the same as a pig. (Martin 1827(I): 107-8)*

Mariner notes that "When Captain Cook visited these islands, cannibalism was scarcely thought of amongst them, but the Fiji people soon taught them this, as well as the art of war" (ibid., 108-9).

Mariner also witnessed a second instance of cannibalism. Sixty men
had been killed in a siege of fortress by King Finow, and after they had
been dedicated to various local gods, the nine or ten bodies belonging
to the enemy:

> ...*were conveyed to the waterside, and there disposed of in different
> ways. Two or three were hung up on a tree; a couple were burnt;
> three were cut open from motives of curiosity, to see whether their
> insides were sound and entire [the liver of those guilty of sacrilege
> was supposed to become diseased], and to practise surgical operations
> upon, hereafter to be described; and lastly, two or three were cut up
> to be cooked and eaten, of which about forty men partook. This was
> the second instance of cannibalism that Mr Mariner had witnessed;
> but the natives of these islands are not to be called cannibals on this
> account. So far from its being a general practice, when these men
> returned to Neafoo after their inhuman repast, most persons who
> knew it, particularly women, avoided them, saying* Iá-whé moe ky-
> tangata, *"Away! You are a man-eater". (ibid., 172-73)*

Despite the initial circumstances of his capture, Mariner established
very friendly relations with the Tongans, whom he clearly liked, and
was an intelligent, well-qualified and fair-minded observer. Modern
anthropologists are quite justified in accepting his evidence, particularly as it is supported by many other observers of the period.

Another good test of Arens's scholarship is his analysis of accounts
of cannibalism in South America, of which a book published in 1557
by Hans Staden, a sixteenth-century German sailor, is given close
attention:

> *Hans Staden [was] an extraordinary fellow who visited the South
> American coast in the mid-sixteenth century as a common seaman on
> a Portuguese trading ship. Through a series of misfortunes, including
> shipwreck, he was soon captured by the Tupinamba Indians. As a*

result of his ill luck, the Tupinamba have come down to us today as man-eaters par excellence. *(22)*

Arens's most serious charge against Staden is that he had little or no command of the Tupi language which, if true, would completely discredit his account of them:

There are also the matters of language and ability to recollect to be considered. In one instance, the narrator ruefully mentions being unable to communicate his plight to a Frenchman who visited his captors' settlement. Apparently he had no facility in the language of his fellow European. However, Staden is able to provide the details of numerous conversations among the Indians themselves, even though he was with them for a relatively limited period. He is particularly adept at recounting verbatim the Indian dialogue on the very first day of his captivity, as they discussed among themselves how, when, and where they would eat Staden. Obviously, he could not have understood the language at the time, and was reconstructing the scene as he imagined it nine years before. The later dialogues in the text must also have been a reconstruction, since there is no indication he kept notes, even if he could write. In one scene, which stands as a testimony to Staden's memory and piety, he repeats the psalm "Out of the deep have I cried unto thee." The Indians respond: "See how he cries; now he is sorrowful indeed"(67). One would have to assume that the Indians also had a flair for languages in order to understand and respond to Staden's German so quickly. In summary, there was great opportunity for a certain degree of embellishment by the author, as well as by his colleagues in the eventual publishing venture. (25-6)

Donald Forsyth, a leading authority on Brazilian ethnohistory, comments:

Arens's implication (1979: 25) that, because Staden couldn't speak the language of his "fellow European", he couldn't speak Tupi either,

*makes about as much sense as arguing that because an individual
has no facility in Russian, he couldn't possibly have any in Portuguese
either." (Forsyth 1985: 21)*

It is actually obvious from Staden's own account that he understood
Tupi perfectly well from the beginning:

*For example, on the very day of his capture he explained (Staden
1928: 65): "The savages asked me whether their enemies the Tuppin
Ikins had been there that year to take the birds during the nesting
season. I told them [emphasis added] that the Tuppin Ikins had been
there, but they proposed to visit the island to see for themselves...." If
Staden did not speak Tupi at the time of his capture, then there is no
way that he could have told them anything, since it is hardly likely
that his captors spoke German or Portuguese. (ibid., 21)*

It is in fact very probable that Staden had learnt Tupi well before
his capture, since he had lived on the coast of Brazil for two years
with a number of other Europeans before he fell into the hands of
the Tupinamba. During this time there was constant contact with
local Indians who spoke the Tupi language, which was common to
a number of tribes besides the Tupinamba. As Forsyth says, "Tupi
was the *lingua franca* of Brazil at this time (and for a long time to
come). The Europeans learned to speak Tupi, rather than the Tupians
learning French or Portuguese" (ibid., 22-3). After a year Staden and
other Europeans reached the Portuguese settlement of Sao Vicente. He
worked for the Portuguese for a year, during which he was given a Tupi-
speaking slave who worked for him on a daily basis, giving him ample
opportunity in itself to learn the language.

Arens is also entirely mistaken when he claims that the Tupi would
have had to understand German when responding to Staden's singing
of a psalm:

*[T]his is simply not so. Staden (1928: 67) actually says: "So in
mighty fear and terror I bethought me of matters which I had never*

dwelt upon before, and considered with myself how dark is the vale of sorrows in which we have our being. Then, weeping, I began in the bitterness of my heart to sing the Psalm: 'Out of the depths have I cried unto thee.' Whereupon the savages rejoiced and said: 'See how he cries: Now he is sorrowful indeed' [emphasis added]". It is not to the German words of the psalm that the Indians respond, rather to the fact that Staden was weeping. (Forsyth 1985: 23-4)

Arens also refers to:

...a small paragraph which curiously informs the reader that "the savages have not the art of counting beyond five". Consequently, they often have to resort to their fingers and toes. In those instances when higher mathematics are involved extra hands and feet are called in to assist in the enumeration. What the author is attempting to convey in his simple way with this addendum is that the Tupinamba lack culture in the sense of basic intellectual abilities. The inability to count is to him supportive documentation for the idea that these savages would resort to cannibalism. To Staden and many others, eating human flesh implies an animal nature which would be accompanied by the absence of other traits of "real" human beings who have a monopoly on culture. (Arens 1979: 23-4)

Chagnon (1977: 74) states that the Yanomamo only have words for one and two, and I record that the same is true of the Tauade; neither of us, however, was trying to insinuate that the Yanomamo and the Tauade were therefore subhuman animals, and Forsyth adds that "Arens completely ignores the fact that Staden's statement concerning Tupinamba enumeration is correct. Ancient Tupi had no terms for numbers beyond four. Larger numbers were expressed in circumlocutions, often involving fingers and toes" (Forsyth 1985: 19). If Arens were better informed he would know that very restricted number systems are often found among hunter-gatherers and simple cultivators, and this condescending, *ad hominem* attack on Staden tells us much more about Arens's prejudices than about Staden's.

Finally, Arens tries to argue that later authors who at first sight appear to confirm Staden's account of cannibalistic ceremonies were in fact simply plagiarising him. Forsyth, however, dismisses the claim of plagiarism entirely:

> *Arens's (1979: 28-30) whole argument is based on the similarities in the accounts of Staden, Lery (1974: 196), Thevet (1971: 61-63), Knivet (1906: 222), and Casas (1971: 68) with respect to the verbal exchange between the victim and executioner before an enemy was killed, cooked, and eaten. His argument is as follows:*

> *In his chapter on killing and eating the victim, Staden supplies some further Indian dialogue which he translates for his readers. He states that the Indian who is about to slay the prisoner says to him: "I am he that will kill you, since you and yours have slain and eaten many of my friends." The prisoner replies: "When I am dead I shall still have many to avenge my death" [Staden 1928: 161]. Dismissing the linguistic barrier momentarily, ... the presentation of the actual words of the characters lends an aura of authenticity to the events. However, if similar phrases begin make their appearance in the accounts of others who put themselves forward eyewitnesses to similar deeds, then the credibility of the confirmation process diminishes (Arens 1979: 28-29). Arens cites the other authors to show the similar phraseology used in describing the execution scene. Hence his whole case for plagiarism is similarities in two sentences in works that are book length in most instances (see Riviere 1980: 204).*

> *As it turns out, however, when even these two sentences are examined in the context of what we know about the cannibalistic rites themselves, and about how and when the accounts were produced, Arens's argument evaporates. An example from our own literate society should suffice to show why this is so. If several different observers wrote a description of the Pledge of Allegiance ceremony, which takes place*

daily in schools all over the nation, we should hardly be surprised to find considerable similarity, since what is said is an essential element in the ceremony. But according to Arens's logic, we would have to conclude that the writers were all copying one another. But the Pledge of Allegiance is not a random event in the daily activities of American school-children. It is, rather, a ritual charged with symbolic meaning. In such a ritual the repetition of behavior and utterance is an integral part of the ceremony…. The verbal exchanges cited by Arens between executioner and victim were not simply random babblings, but highly ritualized exchanges constrained by custom and belief at the very climax of the ceremony, as virtually all of the accounts make patently clear. (Forsyth 1985: 27-8)

Forsyth also points out that Arens ignores a wealth of Jesuit sources that provide eyewitness accounts of cannibalism, the confiscation of cooked (and preserved) human flesh from the Indians, so that they would not eat it, the confiscation of bodies from Indians who were about to eat them, or persuading them to bury the bodies rather than eating them, in one case after the body was already roasted, and the successful rescue of prisoners before they could be killed and eaten:

Whatever the reliability of the better-known sources may be, the Jesuit sources are unimpeachable in this matter, because they avoid all of the alleged weaknesses of the accounts referred to by Arens. They are not copies of Staden, Lery, or Thevet; many of the letters and reports were written before these authors even arrived in Brazil. Moreover, many of the Jesuits did speak the Tupi tongue, even writing dictionaries and grammars to help others learn the language, and lived in Indian villages for extended periods of time. In addition, details of the various Jesuit accounts often differ sufficiently from one another to rule out plagiarism. (Forsyth 1983: 171)

Just as Forsyth claims that Arens ignores a wide range of original sources, particularly those of the Jesuits, Neil Whitehead (1984) also documents Arens's similar failure to consult Jesuit sources with regard to the separate issue of Carib cannibalism.

So far, we have been considering accounts of cannibalism that involve the eating of enemy prisoners, usually killed or captured in warfare. Cross-culturally this appears to be the basic form of cannibalism; there seems little evidence that shortage of protein had anything to do with it, as materialists like Marvin Harris supposed; and many primitive societies were as strongly opposed to cannibalism as we are. There is, however, a different type of cannibalism, conventionally known as "endo-cannibalism", in which the relatives of a deceased person eat the corpse, or part of it, as a mortuary rite. Roy Wagner gives a detailed account of this among the Daribi of the New Guinea Highlands (1967: 145-7), and to a very limited extent the Tauade also practised this:

When a person died and his body had rotted in the tseetsi *[a raised basket] or in the ground, the bones were taken by his relatives and washed in a stream. The skull in particular was washed out with water introduced through the* foramen magnum, *with which the remains of the brain were flushed away. The children of the deceased are said to have drunk this water. (Hallpike 1977: 158)*

Arens, however, is obliged to be just as dismissive of endo-cannibalism as he is of cannibalism in general, and occupies many pages in particular trying to discredit the accounts of this practice among the Fore of New Guinea, which became world-famous through its association with two Nobel Prize winners. Most people would probably consider the Fore case a major obstacle to his theory, and Arens's attempts to dismiss it are excellent examples of the quality of his research. Patrol reports in the Fore area from the early 1950s onwards began describing a disease that became known as *kuru*. Its symptoms were trembling, difficulty in walking and co-ordination, mood changes, and slurred speech, leading to unconsciousness and death usually within a year or less from the first symptoms appearing. (The word *kuru* itself referred to the casuarina tree, whose quivering leaves were seen by the Fore as similar to that of the victims' limbs.) The American physician Carleton Gajdusek happened to be in the area and was told about the disease by Dr Vincent Zigas. The anthropologist Ronald Berndt had already studied it, and considered it psycho-somatic, but Gajdusek came to the firm conclusion that it was entirely physical in origin, and in 1957 Gajdusek and Zigas published a paper claiming that it was a newly discovered neurological disease.

Initially it had been supposed that it might be genetic in origin, but this would have required a long evolutionary history and resulted in epidemiological equilibrium, whereas the Fore claimed that it had first appeared around the beginning of the century, thirty years before contact with Europeans, and its incidence had steadily increased throughout the 1940s and 1950s and was now killing very significant numbers of people. The mortality rate in some villages was 35/1000 per annum, and far more women than men were affected (Lipersky 2013: 479). In 1957, for example, approximately 170 women died compared to 35 men (ibid., Fig. 4, 476). In 1961 the anthropologists Robert and Shirley Glasse (later Lindenbaum) carried out fieldwork on the Fore, with the specific purpose of seeing if victims were close relatives, as the genetic hypothesis predicted, but discovered that they were not. They also made special enquiries into the endo-cannibalistic practices of the Fore, which had been suppressed some years before their work. In the late 1930s and 1940s, many gold miners, Protestant missionaries, and government officials (in other words, Arens's usual "basket of deplorables" in this scenario), had already become familiar with the presence of endo-cannibalism among Eastern Highland tribes (Lipersky 2013: 475). The Glasses made their own enquiries from informants and were able to reconstruct the ways in which this had been carried out on the body of a deceased relative:

> *When a body was considered for human consumption, none of it was discarded except the bitter gall bladder. In the deceased's old sugar-*

cane garden, maternal kin dismembered the corpse with a bamboo knife and stone axe. They first removed hands and feet, then cut open the arms and legs to strip the muscles. Opening the chest and belly, they avoided rupturing the gall bladder, whose bitter content would ruin the meat. After severing the head, they fractured the skull to remove the brain. Meat, viscera, and brain were all eaten. Marrow was sucked from cracked bones, and sometimes the pulverized bones themselves were cooked and eaten with green vegetables. In North Fore but not in the South, the corpse was buried for several days, then exhumed and eaten when the flesh had "ripened" and the maggots could be cooked as a separate delicacy. (Lindenbaum 2013: 224)

They also found that:

Some elderly men rarely ate human flesh, and small children residing with their mothers ate what their mothers gave them. Youths, who were initiated around the age of ten, moved to the men's house, where they began to observe the cultural practices and dietary taboos that defined masculinity. Consuming the dead was considered appropriate for adult women but not men, who feared the pollution and physical depletion associated with eating a corpse. The epidemiological information provided by Gajdusek and Zigas in 1957—that kuru *occurred among women, children of both sexes, and a few elderly men—seemed to match perfectly the Fore rules for human consumption. (Lindenbaum 2015: 104-5)*

Which it did. To cut a long story short, Gajdusek was joined in his research by Stanley Prusiner, a biologist who, like Gajdusek, received the Nobel Prize. The genetic basis of *kuru* had been rejected, and Gajdusek had shown that the disease could be transmitted to chimpanzees exposed to infected material, which suggested to him that the disease was carried by a slow virus. Prusiner, however, showed that *kuru* was actually caused by prions, defective protein molecules which contain no genetic material, and was a spongiform encephalitis in the same family as Creutzfeldt-Jakob disease. The point about prions was that, whereas a slow virus would allow *kuru* to be spread simply by contact, prions required the actual consumption of brain matter, and the obvious occasions for this were the Fore mortuary ceremonies in which the women ate the brains of the deceased. With the demise of cannibalism the incidence of *kuru* fell steadily over the years, and by 1982 there were very few deaths, and the sex ratios were now equal (Lipersky 2013: Fig. 4, 476). The disease is now considered extinct.

While Arens admitted that "it is impossible to prove that cannibalism is not a factor in the *kuru* syndrome", he nevertheless was not convinced: the evidence was circumstantial, there were contradictions in the ethnography, and the same material lent itself to alternate explanations (Arens 1979: 112). He points out that Fore cannibalism had never been observed by an outsider, and that the anthropologists were uncertain when it had been abolished. "As a result, Glasse and Lindenbaum relied upon Berndt's idiosyncratic discussion of the material, the fact that the Fore had a reputation among surrounding groups for eating their dead, the odd report that someone had eaten someone else and the belief among the males that 'the great majority of women' were cannibals" (109). Of this belief about the Fore women he says: "Rather than uncritically accepting the native view that only women and children are cannibals, it would seem reasonable to question whether or not this might be a symbolic statement about females, in a culture area renowned for sexual antagonism and opposition." (110). He goes on, "Another reasonable suspicion of the cannibalism hypothesis is aroused by the fact that among the Fore each death is followed by a mortuary feast involving the slaughter of pigs and distribution of the meat and vegetables.... This period of an abundance of animal protein would seem to be the least likely time to resort to cannibalism" (111).

With regard to the transmission of the disease, which by 1979 had been accepted as related to the Creutzfeldt-Jakob family, he remarks that no one has suggested that such diseases "are transmitted in the western world by cannibalism. However, such a hypothesis presents

no problem when the affected population is the inhabitants of the
New Guinea highlands. This is consistent with the general theoretical
tone of much of the anthropological literature on this area, which
effectively diminishes the cultural achievements of the inhabitants"
(112). With regard to the initial appearance of the disease he says,
"Surprisingly enough, no one has seriously considered the idea that the
presence of Europeans in the area was responsible for the outbreak of
the epidemic at the turn of the century. The arrival of the first two
Europeans in 1932 does not deny the possible entry of the disease
years before through indirect means and intermediaries" (113). He
also points out the important social changes that have occurred since
European contact, such as the disuse of the men's house and men
moving into live with their wives and children: "In the light of the
obvious cultural rearrangements and new experiences, it is odd that
scientific researchers have seized on a correlation between something
which was never seen and another phenomenon studied and measured
so meticulously" (113).

Arens's hilarity at the racist idea of Creutzfeld-Jacob disease being
transmitted by cannibalism turned out to be misplaced, however, since
it was cattle cannibalism in the form of brain and spinal cord matter
from diseased animals being included in cattle feed that led, a few
years later, to the spread of BSE in Britain. Bovine Spongiform
Encephalopathy, or Mad Cow Disease, was a prion disease that also
infected a number of humans in the form of vCJD, variant Creutzfeldt-
Jakob Disease, and led to a ban on the export of British beef in 1996.

In 1997, in "Man is off the menu", he added a further refinement
to his "refutation" of Fore cannibalism, which is worth quoting as an
example of his methods of scholarly disputation:

> *There was a particularly notable agreement [among anthropologists]
> that cannibals did exist, however, until practically yesterday, in the
> highlands of New Guinea, the "final frontier" of western cultural
> contact. In this instance many smugly noted that the evidence for*

cannibalism emerged from medical research rather than from the usual less reliable forms of documentation. In the light of the exalted position of science, how could any rational person doubt this research? I discovered, with perhaps even more smugness, that one could. The story began in 1957, with the arrival in New Guinea of D. Carleton Gajdusek, an American research paediatrician on his way home from a fellowship year in Australia. Why he opted to visit this part of the world did not become clear until recently. However, the eventual results of the sojourn proved important for both medical science and for Dr Gajdusek. Eventually, he would receive the Nobel prize for medicine, and then, later, be arrested and plead guilty to the sexual abuse of minors in the US. He adopted a number of boys from part of New Guinea well known for institutionalised male homosexuality between youngsters and adults. Laudatory reports of Gajdusek's charity, including references to his bringing a number of the lads to the Nobel ceremonies, were recounted in the media. (Arens 1997: 16)

Gajdusek's subsequent criminal conviction related to boys of a different people from the Fore and had nothing whatever to do with his *kuru* research, and therefore provides Arens with no grounds for doubting it, smugly or otherwise. Arens, of course, as we might expect, makes no reference in his article to Prusiner's work and the crucial association of brain-matter with prions which was conclusive support for the cannibalistic thesis, and by 1997 had been well-established.

I leave it to my readers to decide if they find these various arguments of Arens even a remotely adequate response to the facts presented on Fore cannibalism. Shirley Lindenbaum comments that "Although discredited today, the denial of cannibalism was kept alive during the 1980s and 1990s by a generational shift in the human sciences, glossed as postmodernism, which studied metaphor and representation, providing new life for the idea that cannibalism was nothing more than a colonizing trope and stratagem, a calumny used by colonizers to justify their predatory behavior" (Lindenbaum 2015: 108).

To sum up, then, Arens's charge that anthropologists engage in "manipulating the data to generate a foregone conclusion" where "academic standards seem to function as an almost forgotten ideal", actually turns out to be a very accurate description of his own book, and Marshall Sahlins, who has done more than most to refute it, may be allowed the last word:

It all follows a familiar American pattern of enterprising social science journalism: Professor X puts out some outrageous theory, such as the Nazis really didn't kill the Jews, human civilization comes from another planet, or there is no such thing as cannibalism. Since facts are plainly against him, X's main argument consists of the expression, in the highest moral tones, of his own disregard for all available evidence to the contrary. He rises instead to the more elevated analytical plane of ad hominem attack on the authors of the primary sources and those credulous enough to believe them. All this provokes Y and Z to issue a rejoinder, such as this one. X now becomes 'the controversial Professor X' and his book is respectfully reviewed by non-professionals in Time, Newsweek, *and* The New Yorker. *There follow appearances on radio, TV, and in the columns of the daily newspapers. (Sahlins 1979)*

Notes

1. The class of stupid, ignorant people.
2. For Cook's actual Journal entry see J. C. Beaglehole, ed., 1969. *The Voyage of the Resolution and Adventure 1772-1775* (Cambridge: The University Press for the Hakluyt Society), pp. 292-293.
3. But Sahlins also explains that the authorship of this account might have been mistakenly attributed to Endicott:

   It could be that Endicott indeed did not see the event, insofar as he may well not be the author of the contested text. The original of that text, reprinted and signed by Endicott as an appendix to his book, is an article that appeared in The Danvers Courier newspaper on 16 August 1845, under the byline "By an Eye Witness". The Peabody Museum, where the article is archived, apparently attributes it to a different member of the Glide's *crew, Henry Fowler (of Danvers) with whose papers it is included (Fowler, PMB 225). Indeed, a simple "F" is inscribed at the bottom of the original newspaper article (Sahlins 2003: 3, n.3) But whether Endicott or Fowler provided the actual account, it is confirmed by numerous other contemporary records.*

So all languages aren't equally complex after all

1. All languages are born equal

People outside the specialised sphere of linguistics have generally taken it for granted that, just as there are simple and complex cultures there would correspondingly be simple and complex languages. But for most of the last hundred years linguists have claimed that even if some cultures are simpler than others, All Languages are Equally Complex: ALEC, or uniformitarianism. "There are Stone Age societies, but there is no such thing as a Stone Age Language. Earlier in this [20th] century the anthropological linguist Edward Sapir wrote, 'When it comes to linguistic form, Plato walks with the Macedonian swineherd, Confucius with the head-hunting savage of Assam' " (Pinker 2015: 25). Or again, "[N]o sign of evolution from a simpler to a more complex state of development can be found in any of the thousands of languages known to exist or to have existed in the past" (Lyons 1977 (I): 85, and see Lyons 1970: 21-22). Or, as a fairly recent linguistics textbook has said, "All languages are equally complex and equally capable of expressing any idea" (Fromkin et al. 2010: 34)[1].

Indeed, many would also dispute that there are "Stone Age" societies, and argue that non-industrial peoples had systems of language, knowledge, and culture as complex and valid in their world view as our own. As one anthropologist has said, "All people are essentially equal in their ability to become cultured, and all people encounter approximately the same amount of information in the process of enculturation. Thus it is untenable to maintain that one culture is 'higher' or more complex than another. In reality, there are no simple or primitive cultures: all cultures are equally complex and equally modern" (Hamill 1990: 106). Or again, "[People] think the same thoughts, no matter what kind of grammatical system they use; and they express the same kinds of thoughts, regardless of the grammatical tools they have: past, present and future events, cause and effect relationships, social relationships, hypothetical questions, and so forth" (Jackendoff and Wittenberg 2014: 66).

There is no doubt that egalitarian ideology has been a very powerful motivation for this belief. "The reason why linguistics was worth studying, for many descriptivists [such as Sapir and Boas], was that it helped to demonstrate that 'all men are brothers'—Mankind is not divided into a group of civilized nations or races who think in subtle and complex ways, and another group of primitive societies with crudely simple languages" (Sampson 2009a: 4). But while linguists could justifiably point out that some languages spoken by tribal peoples could be grammatically and phonologically more complex than some European languages, there was no systematic attempt to find evidence for the general theory of uniformitarianism. Hockett, for example, simply maintained that the total grammatical complexity of any language was more or less bound to be the same as any other's, "since all languages have about equally complex jobs to do" (1958: 180), a very strange assumption indeed, as we shall see.

When the traditional "descriptive" linguistics of Sapir and others[2] was replaced by the generative linguistics (which became Universal Grammar) of Chomsky and his school, the dogma of equal complexity remained the same:

If we come forward to the generative linguistics of the last forty-odd years, we find that linguists are no longer interested in discussing whether language structure reflects a society's cultural level, because

*generative linguists do not see language structure as an aspect of
human culture. Except for minor details, they believe it is determined
by human biology, and in consequence there is no question of some
languages being structurally more complex than other languages—
in essence they are all structurally identical to one another. Of
course there are some parameters which are set differently in different
languages: adjectives precede nouns in English but follow nouns in
French. But choice of parameter settings is a matter of detail that
specifies how an individual language expresses a universal range of
logical distinctions—it does not allow languages to differ from one
another with respect to the overall complexity of the set of distinctions
expressed, and it does not admit any historical evolution with respect
to that complexity.… The innate cognitive machinery which is central
to the generative concept of language competence is taken to be too
comprehensive to leave room for significant differences with respect to
complexity. (Sampson 2009a: 6-7)*

2. The aims of this paper

In the general context of what we know about biological, social and
cultural development the claim that all languages are equally complex
is extremely odd. Biological organisms have obviously evolved increasingly complex forms, in the sense of having an increasing number of
component parts, specialisation of function, and hierarchical structures, and the same process can be observed in social organization,
culture, and technology. Why, then, should language be any different? As a social anthropologist who conducted several years' fieldwork
among the Konso of Ethiopia (Hallpike 2008), and the Tauade of
Papua New Guinea (Hallpike 1977), it has always been obvious to
me from personal experience that claims that "all cultures are equally
complex" are simply untrue, and my belief is supported by a vast
ethnographic literature (see Hallpike 1992 for a summary). I also
applied Piagetian developmental psychology to the data of small-scale,

non-literate societies with subsistence economies ("primitive societies") in *The Foundations of Primitive Thought* (1979) and *Ethical Thought in Increasingly Complex Societies* (2016). These assembled a wealth of evidence to show that modes of thought about the natural world, causality, classification, notions of the self, society, and ethics do indeed follow a developmental pathway, and that the thought worlds of modern literate urban societies are very different from those found in primitive societies. This work also refuted the standard anthropological dogma that individual psychology cannot be used to explain collective representations, and showed that since culture can only be transmitted through individuals, their psychology has to be an integral part in the formation of these collective representations.

Language is perhaps the pre-eminent example of a collective representation, although not being a linguist I did not feel professionally competent to challenge the doctrine of ALEC. But I have recently been encouraged[3] to find that it, together with Chomsky's Universal Grammar, are increasingly being rejected by linguists, and I have tried here to summarise their main conclusions for the benefit of anthropologists. The main theme of this paper is therefore a critique of the theory that language can be a genetically based "organ", "instinct", or "module", and aims to show that, while clearly the language *capacity* depends on some unique and evolved qualities of the human brain, the characteristics of natural languages cannot be understood unless they are also placed in the context of social relations and the ways in which these have developed in the course of history.

3. Chomsky and Universal Grammar

Chomsky began developing his theory of Universal Grammar or UG in the 1950s to demonstrate that language, or more specifically grammar (syntax + morphology), is a distinct cognitive function that is innate and genetically specified, a mental "organ" with very detailed characteristics like the heart or the eye. In adopting this approach Chomsky was in perfectly orthodox scientific company, since the prevailing view of the brain was that known as "localizationalism": "the idea that the brain is like a complex machine, made up of parts, each of which performs a specific mental function and exists in a genetically predetermined or hardwired *location*—hence the name" (Doidge 2007: 12). This view of language was highly compatible with subsequent developments in computer science by which it could be represented as a specific computational programme, and later also formed close links with "evolutionary psychology", that grew up with socio-biology in the 1980s. This claimed that every mental function was a "module", an encapsulated computational device evolved to solve all the various problems that our ancestors had encountered during the Pleistocene, whether it be detecting cheaters, child-care, mathematics, tool-use or of course language.

Chomsky used the theory of Universal Grammar very effectively to refute Skinner's Behaviourist claim (Chomsky 1959) that speech could be explained without any reference to a supposed "mind", but purely as the product of operant conditioning in which items of "verbal behaviour" were emitted in response to particular stimuli, and then subject to reinforcement. Chomsky pointed out however that children were able to utter grammatically well-formed statements that they had never heard before, and could attain correct grammar without being constantly corrected, or even corrected at all. Behaviourist theory was quite incapable of answering these objections which were decisive. For Chomsky, then, the basic justifications for saying that the capacity for language must be an innate module or organ, a computational mechanism, was the argument from the poverty of the input together with lack of correction, and ease of acquisition in childhood (Pinker 2015: 40).

[H]uman cognitive systems, when seriously investigated, prove to be no less marvellous and intricate than the physical structures that develop in the life of the organism. Why, then, should we not study the

acquisition of a cognitive structure such as language more or less as we study some complex bodily organ? (Chomsky 1975: 10). What many linguists call "universal grammar" may be regarded as a theory of innate mechanisms, an underlying biological matrix that provides a framework within which the growth of language proceeds. (Chomsky 1980a: 187)

For Chomsky the basic or defining element of the language organ is recursion, recursion not simply in the sense of iteration, repeating the same process indefinitely, but in the sense of taking the output of one stage in a process and making it the input of the next stage:

…lying at the heart of language: its capacity for limitless expressive power, captured by the notion of discrete infinity. …no species other than humans has a comparable capacity to recombine meaningful units into an unlimited variety of larger structures *[my emphasis], each differing systematically in meaning. (Hauser, Chomsky & Fitch 2002: 1576)*

Recursion, then, in this sense is the structure-building process *par excellence*, particularly the process linguists refer to as embedding, in which one clause is included or subordinated in another:

Natural languages go beyond purely local structure [e.g., phrases] by including a capacity for recursive embedding of phrases within phrases, *which can lead to statistical regularities that are separated by an arbitrary number of words or phrases [e.g., in the sentence "The man whom you saw yesterday speaks French" the subject "man" is separated from the verb "speaks" by the four words of the relative clause]. Such long-distance, hierarchical relationships are found in* all natural languages *[my emphases]. (ibid., 1577)*

Linguists have generally made a clear distinction between iteration and recursion, whose distinctive property is the embedding of phrases or sentences within larger phrases or sentences.

Unfortunately, Chomsky in the same paper also says that recursion "takes a finite set of elements and yields a potentially infinite array of discrete expressions" (ibid., 1571) and had previously substantially revised his notion of UG by reducing it to the fundamental principle of Merge. This simply "takes a pair of syntactic objects and replaces them by a new combined syntactic object" (Chomsky 1995: 226), and appears in fact to blur substantially the distinction between recursion and iteration. Bickerton (2009: 536-7) indeed claims that iteration in the form of Merge can achieve the same results as recursion in the traditional sense. Some linguists have even concluded that any expression of more than two words must involve recursion-as-iteration, which is singularly unhelpful. This is a debate that one must therefore leave to linguists; but the fact remains that the concept of recursion as requiring embedding, subordinate clauses, is an extremely important cognitive process that is highly relevant to the notion of linguistic complexity and is also testable:

> [T]he core idea of recursion is clear and unambiguous, and it is the simplest and most powerful route to the type of unbounded expressive power that is a crucial feature of mathematics or language.... Recursive embedding of phrases within phrases is an important tool allowing language users to express any concept that can be conceived, to whatever degree of accuracy or abstraction is needed. The achievements of human science, philosophy, literature, law, and of culture in general depend, centrally, upon there being no limit to how specific (or how general) the referents of our linguistic utterances can be. (Fitch 2010: 89)

For the purposes of this paper I shall therefore ignore the implications of Merge, and concentrate on the theory that language is genetically based in a "language organ", and that its most important manifestation is recursive embedding.

But, unlike the earlier descriptivist linguists like Boas and Sapir, who made intensive field-studies of the languages of the Native Peoples of

North America, Chomsky based his theories essentially on English. He defended this as follows:

> *I have not hesitated to propose a general principle of linguistic structure on the basis of observation of a single language. The inference is legitimate, on the assumption that humans are not specifically adapted to learn one rather than another human language, say English rather than Japanese. Assuming that the genetically determined language faculty is a common human possession, we may conclude that a principle of language is universal if we are led to postulate it as a "precondition" for the acquisition of a single language. (Chomsky 1980b: 48)*

In rather the same way, perhaps, Newtonian physics might defend itself by saying that although it was based on the study of only one solar system, the laws inferred from this were universal. But in the course of time it became clear that languages from non-literate peoples in particular departed in major ways from this English-derived model, and the language organ now includes what have come to be known as "Principles and Parameters". "Principles" are the *universals* of language, whereas "Parameters" respond to linguistic *differences*: they are the fundamental options or possibilities in generating the grammar of a language: "...also specified are the relevant principles and parameters common to the species and part of the initial state of the organism; these principles and parameters make up part of the theory of grammar or Universal Grammar, and they belong to the genotype" (Anderson and Lightfoot 2000: 14). One parameter, for example, is word order, and it seems that 95% of the world's languages are either SVO, like English, or SOV like German. Another is the "Null-Subject" parameter: with English verbs it is not permissible to omit the subject and say simply "is raining": the form "it is raining" is required, even though "it" has a purely grammatical function here. In Italian, however, the form *"piove"*, "is raining" is quite correct, and this null-subject parameter also explains a number of other related aspects of the grammars of English and Italian, and many other languages (Baker 2001: 36-44)[4].

So we now find very strong claims for the scope of the "language organ", for example:

> *All languages have a vocabulary in the thousands or tens of thousands, sorted into part-of-speech categories including noun and verb. Words are organized into phrases according to the X-bar system (nouns are found inside N-bars, which are found inside noun phrases, and so on). The higher levels of phrase structure include auxiliaries ... which signify tense, modality, aspect, and negation. Nouns are marked for case and assigned semantic roles by the mental dictionary entry of the verb or other predicate. Phrases can be moved from their deep structure positions, leaving a gap or "trace", by a structure-dependent movement rule, thereby forming questions, relative clauses, passives, and other widespread constructions. New word structures can be created and modified by derivational and inflectional rules. Inflectional rules primarily mark nouns for case and number, and mark verbs for tense, aspect, mood, voice, negation, and agreement with subjects and objects in number, gender, and person. (Pinker 2015: 235-6)*

And some linguists make equally strong claims for the scope of a genetic basis of language: "Much remains to be done, but ... [e]ventually, the growth of language in a child will be viewed as similar to the growth of hair: just as hair emerges with a certain level of light, air, and protein, so, too, a biologically regulated language organ necessarily emerges under exposure to a random speech community" (Anderson and Lightfoot 2000: 21).

Finally, we need to consider Chomsky's explanation for how such a genetically based "language organ" could have developed in the first place. Strikingly, unlike Pinker and many others, he does not believe that it was the product of natural selection at all. This is because he also dismisses the general assumption that the origins of language must have been in the context of *communication*, that, if you like, there is no point in speaking if there is no one else who can understand what is being said. He maintains that the "language organ" resulted from a major genetic mutation, probably within the last 100,000 years:

> *Within some small group from which we are descended, a rewiring of the brain took place in some individual, call him* Prometheus, *yielding the operation of unbounded Merge, applying to concepts with intricate (and little understood) properties.... Prometheus's language provides him with an intricate array of structured expressions with interpretations of the kind illustrated: duality of semantics, operator-variable constructions.... Prometheus had many advantages: capacities for complex thought, planning, interpretation, and so on. The capacity would then be transmitted to offspring, coming to predominate.... At that stage there would be an advantage to externalization, so the capacity might come to be linked as a secondary process to the S[ensory]M[otor] system, for externalization and interaction, including communication [through speech].* (Chomsky 2010: 59)

Prometheus's mutation, in other words, initially applied only to Inner thought, Mentalese, I[nternal]-Language, not to E[xternal]-Language or real speech. This refers to the fact that there has to be a distinction between thoughts and words: we are all aware, for example, of searching for just the right word to express an idea we have, of feeling we have not expressed our meaning very well, of objecting to someone's theory before we have actually put our objection into words, and so on. But it is not in the least obvious how this mutation could have conferred any capacity for "complex thought" in the absence of any social interaction, or any language in which to exchange these thoughts. Chomsky nevertheless maintains that the mutation in question was about our increased ability to think with precision, not to communicate any better, and that this in itself would have been of sufficient adaptive advantage to Prometheus to ensure the propagation of the language gene:

Salvador Luria was the most forceful advocate of the view that communicative needs would not have provided "any great selective pressure to produce a system such as language," with its crucial relation to "the development of abstract or productive thinking." The same idea was taken up by his fellow Nobel laureate François Jacob, who suggested that "the role of language as a communication system between individuals would have come about only secondarily, as many linguists believe.... The quality of language that makes it unique does not seem to be so much its role in communicating directives for action" or other common features of animal communication, but rather "its role in symbolizing, in evoking cognitive images", in "molding" our notion of reality and yielding our capacity for thought and planning, through its unique property of allowing "infinite combinations of symbols" and therefore "mental creation of possible worlds". (Chomsky 2010: 55)

4. Is a "language organ" actually possible?

There are, unsurprisingly, a number of objections to this view of the language organ and U[niversal] G[rammar]. (As previously mentioned, this is now referred to as the Minimalist principle of unbounded Merge but for simplicity I shall continue to refer to UG.) The first is that it is bizarre to claim that language can be a physical organ in the same sense as the heart or the eye. These have standard forms and functions, which are genetically determined and entirely material in nature, and are also confined to the operation of the body of which they are parts. Language, on the other hand, although having some kind of genetic basis is also, unlike the bodily organs, a *social* phenomenon produced by the interaction of many minds, and is also concerned with the communication of non-material *meaning* between a number of individuals. Like the brain of which it is one function among many, but unlike all the other bodily organs, it is capable of limitless diversity, and it can also develop very different levels of complexity, again unlike all other bodily organs. The idea that language is an organ like the heart or the eye is therefore vastly underdetermined by the evidence.

The next objection is that, when faced with Chomsky's mythical Prometheus, whose ability to master the most complex syntax suddenly appeared fully formed in his brain, we need to remind ourselves of a basic principle of natural selection. This is that a trait can only be selected if it is relevant to the existing circumstances in which an organism is living, not those that might exist in the future. This point was made long ago by A. R. Wallace, the co-formulator of the theory of natural selection with Darwin, and who had extensive first-hand acquaintance with hunter-gatherers of the Amazon and south-east Asia. He noted that on the one hand their mode of life made only very limited intellectual demands, and did not require abstract concepts of number and geometry, space, time, and advanced ethical principles, or music, yet they were potentially capable of mastering the advanced cognitive skills of modern industrial civilisation. Since natural selection can only produce traits that are adapted to existing, and not future, conditions, it "could only have endowed savage man with a brain a little superior to that of an ape, where he actually possesses one little inferior to that of a philosopher" (Wallace 1871: 356). But how could the language organ have developed the capacity for the highly complex syntactic structures involved in, say, modern legal or philosophical arguments tens of thousands of years before they were needed or relevant to the simple lives of hunter-gatherers?

Chomsky, of course, would dismiss Wallace's point on the grounds that the linguistic ability of Prometheus was not produced by natural selection at all, but by an amazing mutation instead. This escape of Prometheus from what might seem an impossible evolutionary situation is about as implausible as the legendary escape of Jack, the hero of a thriller series, from apparently inevitable death by the explanation that "with one bound Jack was free". Evolutionary psychologists such as Pinker naturally disagree fundamentally with Chomsky and maintain that communication was basic, and that language is only one of a large number of "modules" in the brain that have evolved over millions of years through natural selection. According to Pinker, "The mind is organized into modules or mental organs, each with a specialized design that makes it an expert in one arena of interaction with the world. The modules" basic logic is specified by our genetic program" (Pinker 1997: 21), and language is just one module among very many. These modules are supposed to have been shaped by natural selection during the several million years of hunter-gatherer life the Pleistocene in East Africa, the "environment of evolutionary adaptation" or EEA (about which, incidentally, we know virtually nothing). So:

> *Just as one can now flip open Gray's Anatomy to any page and find an intricately detailed depiction of some part of our evolved species-typical morphology, we anticipate that in 50 or 100 years one will be able to pick up an equivalent work for psychology and find in it detailed information-processing descriptions of the multitude of evolved species-typical adaptations of the human mind, including how they are mapped on to the corresponding neuro-anatomy and how they are constructed by developmental programs. (Tooby and Cosmides 1992: 69)*

Mathematics is another of these alleged modules, and its comparison with the language "organ" is illuminating here. Unlike language, which is both universal and very ancient, mathematics much beyond the level of simple tallying only emerged in the high cultures of recorded history, and its expert practitioners have always been a small minority of any population. According to Pinker, "Mathematics is part of our birthright" (1997: 338), but this is only true in a very rudimentary sense. When collections of objects are less than ten, a wide variety of species such as pigeons, ravens, parrots, rats, monkeys, and chimpanzees can recognise changes in the numbers of objects in a collection, compare the sizes of two collections presented simultaneously, and remember the number of objects presented successively (Koehler 1951,

Pepperberg 1987, Mechner & Guerrekian 1962, Woodruff & Premack 1981, Matsuzawa 1985).

A sense of what has been called "numerosity", then, of the differences in quantities of small size, is widespread, and to this extent the human "mathematical birthright" is not distinguishable from that of many other species. So many simple cultures, especially hunter-gatherers but including some shifting cultivators such as the Tauade of Papua New Guinea (Hallpike 1977), may only have words for single, pair, and many. Indeed, the hunter-gatherer Piraha of South America are described by Everett (2008) as having no number words at all, not even the grammatical distinction between singular and plural, but we shall come back to them in more detail later.

We can get a good idea why this should be so from the example of a Cree hunter from eastern Canada: he was asked in a court case involving land how many rivers there were in his hunting territory, and did not know:

The hunter knew every river in his territory individually and therefore had no need to know how many there were. Indeed, he would know each stretch of each river as an individual thing and therefore had no need to know in numerical terms how long the rivers were. The point of the story is that we count things when we are ignorant of their individual identity [my emphasis]—this can arise when we don't have enough experience of the objects, when there are too many of them to know individually, or when they are all the same, none of which conditions obtain very often for a hunter. If he has several knives they will be known individually by their different sizes, shapes, and specialized uses. If he has several pairs of moccasins they will be worn to different degrees, having been made at different times, and may be of different materials and design. (Denny 1986: 133)

Again, the Tauade, like many peoples of Papua New Guinea, only had words for single, *kone*, and pair, *kupariai*. "Single" and "pair", it should be emphasized, are not the same as one and two: 2 is 1+1, and

3 is 1+1+1, successive elements of a series, but "single" and "pair" are not components of a series but are *configurations* that can take many different forms. For example there are pairs of twins, or a man and a woman, a man and a man, and a woman and a woman, or left and right, or sun and moon, and so on which each have different social and symbolic significance, whereas there can't be different kinds of 1 or 2. Although the Tauade engage in complex transactions of pork exchange they have never needed to use a counting system to keep track of these because each exchange is unique, between different persons, for different purposes and in different circumstances. Here again, like the Cree, *distinctive individual identity* is key to the lack of number and counting. (The Tauade had only recently adopted the Tok Pisin number system based on ten because they had to deal with modern money whose coins and notes have no individual identity.) What needs to be emphasised here, therefore, is that in hunter-gatherer societies especially, it is perfectly possible to survive without the need for verbal numerals or for counting, and that consequently there could have been no selective pressure for arithmetical skills to evolve in the specific conditions of the EEA, and for any specific module to develop. So are we really expected to believe that a mathematics module, with all its capacity to produce modern mathematics, nevertheless did develop but mysteriously sat there in silence, as it were, until the emergence of complex societies?

As we all know, mathematics has only flowered in the last few centuries, far too brief a time-span for natural selection to have had the least effect, and it has developed out of all recognition from the simple counting systems of tribal societies. While the relatively small number of those who excel at mathematics presumably have some genetic advantage over the rest of us, the historical development of mathematics must have depended on a number of more general and pre-existing mental functions that were put to use in the development of mathematics, itself reacting to the changing circumstances of the social milieu.

Evolutionary psychologists like Pinker would reply, of course, that there is indeed a module for mathematics, just as there is for most aspects of mental functioning. For example, Hauser in *Moral Minds* (2008) claims that we have an innate morality module, a "universal moral grammar", basically similar to Chomsky's generative grammar for language. Just as our innate generative grammar allows us to construct a limitless variety of correct sentences, so Hauser proposes that our universal moral grammar has "a capacity that enables each individual to unconsciously and automatically evaluate a limitless variety of actions in terms of principles that dictate what is permissible, obligatory, or forbidden" (ibid., 41). Moral thought, however, evolves in relation to social complexity, as I have shown in detail in *Ethical Thought in Increasingly Complex Societies* (2016) which is incompatible with modularity. How, in any case, did natural selection manage to endow us with a module that could foresee the moral dilemmas we would face in complex industrial societies thousands of years before these had developed?

In short, then, Wallace's argument demonstrates a fatal weakness in all evolutionary psychology which is that natural selection can only improve adaptation to *existing* circumstances, never to those that might arise in the future (and see Hallpike 2011 for a number of other objections). Instead of the adaptationism of natural selection we therefore need to appeal to Stephen J. Gould's notion of "exaptation". Whereas "adaptations" are characteristics evolved under natural selection for the better performance of some task or function, there can also be characteristics that have proved to be useful, but which were not initially selected for such a use:

> *We suggest that such characters, evolved for other usages (or for no function at all) and later "coopted" for their current role, be called* exaptations.... *They are fit for their current role, hence* aptus, *but they were not designed for it, and are therefore not* ad aptus, *or pushed towards fitness. They owe their fitness to features present for other*

reasons, and are therefore fit (aptus) by reason of (ex) *their form.…
Adaptations have functions; exaptations have effects.   (Gould and
Vrba 1982: 6)*

*Most of what the brain now does to enhance our survival lies in the do-
main of exaptation—and does not allow us to make hypotheses about
the selective paths of human history. How much of the evolutionary
literature on human behaviour would collapse if we incorporated
the principle of exaptation into the core of evolutionary thinking?
This collapse would be constructive because it would vastly broaden
our range of hypotheses, and focus attention on current function
and development (all testable propositions) instead of leading us to
unprovable reveries about primal fratricide on the African savanna or
dispatching mammoths at the edge of great ice sheets—a valid subject,
but one better treated in novels. (ibid., 13)*

Or, one might add, reveries about Prometheus on the African savannah as well.

In the years since the inception of UG our knowledge of how the
brain works has increased exponentially, and the whole idea of mental
modules is now distinctly *passé*. For example "…there are many different system organizations that can produce the same kind of behaviour
a strictly modular system does and … they may not be distinguishable from it by any conceivable experimental strategy.… Nonlinear,
interconnected, dynamic systems [such as the brain] are fully capable
of producing the kind of behaviour expected from modular systems"
(Uttal 2001: 182-3).

Indeed, culture itself can modify the way in which the brain operates:

*Neuroplastic research has shown us that every sustained activity ever
mapped—including physical activities, sensory activities, learning,
thinking, and imagining—changes the brain as well as the mind.
Cultural ideas and activities are no exception.   Our brains are
modified by the cultural activities we do—be they reading, studying*

music, or learning new languages. We all have what might be called a culturally modified brain, and as cultures evolve, they continually lead to new changes in the brain. (Doidge 2007: 288)

While there is undoubtedly some cognitive specialisation in the brain, as in the different functions of the two hemispheres (see McGilchrist 2012), there must be a limit to this:

It would simply not be feasible to construct a brain that allocates a specific psychological module to every conceivable event an individual might encounter, as the costs in terms of neural circuitry and information processing would be huge. There is no intrinsic virtue to mental specificity: general solutions will be favoured when they can do a good enough job at with evolutionary theory than domain-specific processes (Laland and Brown 2002: 182-3).

It has often been suggested that language originated either from music or from gesture, and whatever truth there may be in either of these evolutionary theories, there is no doubt that as the brain operates today there are close, and very unmodular, links between these areas and those of speech and language:

The location of grasp in the left hemisphere, close to speech, is not accidental and tells us something. We know from experience that there are many connections between the hand and language. For example, there is clearly a close relationship between spoken language and the wealth of gesture language that often accompanies it. In normal subjects, restricting hand movement produces an adverse effect on the content and fluency of speech.... At the neurophysiological level, too, it turns out that there are similarities between the skills required for hand movement, specifically movement of the right hand.... Manipulospatial abilities may have provided the basis of primitive language, and such abilities and referential language require similar neural mechanisms. The syntactic elements of language may well derive from gesture. (McGilchrist 2012: 111)

Music, too, far from being some trivial side-effect of brain activity, also has fundamental links with language:

In the first place, the "syntax" of music is simpler, less highly evolved than that of language, suggesting an earlier origin. More importantly, observation of the development of language in children confirms that the musical aspects of language do indeed come first. Intonation, phrasing and rhythm develop first; syntax and vocabulary come only later. (ibid., 103)

McGilchrist also points out that music, like gesture, has a profoundly social dimension:

If language began in music, it began in (right hemisphere) functions which are related to empathy and common life, not competition and division; promoting togetherness, or, as I would prefer, "betweenness". By its nature as a means of communication, language is inevitably a shared activity, like music, which begins in the transmission of emotion and promotes cohesion. Human singing is unique: no other creature begins to synchronise the rhythm, or blend the pitch, of its utterances with that of its fellows, in the way that human singing instinctively does. It is not, like birdsong, individualistic in intention and competitive in nature (remember that birdsong, like other instrumental utterances, is grounded in the left hemisphere, not, like human music, in the right). (ibid., 123)

Again, metaphor, and analogy which is its extension, are basic aspects of human thought. "Only the right hemisphere has the capacity to understand metaphor.... Metaphoric thinking is fundamental to our understanding of the world, because it is the only way in which understanding can reach outside the systems of signs to life itself. It is what links language to life" (ibid., 115).

But metaphor and analogy are not computational exercises, nor are the writing of poems, plays, and novels, music, painting or sculpture.

Religion, politics, and social life in general are not computational exercises either, because, as in the arts, there are no problems or clearly defined set of problems that any of these activities has evolved to solve during the Pleistocene; there are no set of rules for doing so; and no agreed criteria for deciding if the output is right or wrong. Fodor himself, who originally popularized the idea of mental modules, emphasizes that analogical thinking in general cannot be modular and has to be global:

> *It is strange that, while everybody thinks that analogical reasoning is an important ingredient in all sorts of cognitive achievements that we prize, nobody knows anything about how it works; not even in the dim, in-a-glass-darkly sort of way in which there are some ideas about how confirmation works. I don't think this is an accident either. In fact, I should like to propose a generalization.... It goes like this: the more global ... a cognitive process is, the less anybody understands it. Very global processes, like analogical reasoning, aren't understood at all. (Fodor 1983: 107)*

Finally, while UG was able to give an explanation of linguistic diversity by the principles and parameters theory, that to the non-linguist at least appears very impressive, it is much harder to see how such a module could possibly account for the *developmental* aspects of language other than, of course by simply denying that they can exist— ALEC. The point here is that if there is a genetically based faculty like language, an "organ of the mind", one would expect it to operate in a unitary fashion with all the parameters set, and not for some aspects of it to take many millennia to emerge when circumstances are right. This is especially true of recursion, supposedly the very heart of the language instinct, yet which as we shall see may be very weakly developed or even non-existent in the simpler languages. If, on the other hand, we find that linguistic complexity does develop in relation to social and cultural complexity, particularly in relation to writing and literacy, then how is it to be distinguished from other aspects of learned behaviour, that are derived from the rest of human culture that has been collectively constructed over a very long period by individuals with the unique general capacities of the human brain? What empirical test would there be, in other words, to distinguish an innate language organ from the product of a *constructive* and *developmental* process of the kind proposed by Piaget?

Fifty years of experience have taught us that knowledge does not result from a mere recording of observations without a structuring activity on the part of the subject. Nor do any a priori or innate cognitive structures exist in man; the functioning of intelligence alone is hereditary and creates structures only through an organization of successive actions performed on objects[5]. Consequently, an epistemology conforming to the data of psychogenesis could be neither empiricist nor preformationist, but could consist only of a constructivism, with a continual elaboration of new operations and structures. The central problem, then, is to understand how such operations come about, and why, even though they result from non-predetermined constructions, they eventually become logically necessary. (Piaget 1980: 23)

It is mental activities, not structures, then, that will be innate, and since language is a linear, one-dimensional mode of communication, we can also expect to find that it will obey certain simple constraints on conveying meaning, that as Greenberg proposed, certain sequences of syntactic elements will give optimal cues for parsing (conveying and extracting meaning). Rather than proposing the unverifiable theory that structures like embedding are "latent" in the language organ, as UG theorists would have it, one would therefore suggest instead a set of functional arguments to account for universal trends in language development that will also be limited in number (Prof. J. Colarusso, personal communication).

5. Linguistic simplicity and linguistic complexity

Pinker gives a useful description of the essential features of human language:

> *The discrete combinatorial system called "grammar" makes human language infinite (there is no limit to the number of complex words or sentences in a language), digital (this infinity is achieved by rearranging discrete elements in particular orders and combinations, not by varying some signal along a continuum like the mercury in a thermometer), and compositional (each of the infinite combinations has a different meaning predictable from the meanings of its parts and the rules and principles arranging them). (Pinker 2015: 332)*

But within this definition, language forms a spectrum from the simple to the complex that is related to the level of sociocultural complexity. There has been a great deal of debate about what we mean by "linguistic complexity", and how it is to be measured, if at all (see in particular Newmayer and Preston 2014). But it is nevertheless possible to observe an important difference between those aspects of grammar that have developmental significance and those that do not. In the second category are, for example: phonology[6]; differences of word order; the presence or absence of case and gender, so that in German there are 16 possible ways of saying the single English word "the"; the distinctions between isolating and synthetic languages (English and Latin), and between these languages and polysynthetic languages such as Mohawk; head-initial and head-final languages (English and Japanese); ergative/absolutive or nominative/ accusative languages (Basque and German), the null-subject parameter (English and Italian), and many others, which can be found all over the world regardless of the social and cultural complexity of their speakers.

On the other hand, there are a number of linguistic features that have strong developmental correlations. First of all we should be clear that, despite the strange claims of some linguists to the contrary, the lexicons of primitive societies, and pre-modern societies for that matter, will be considerably smaller than those typical of modern industrial societies. For example, we can say anything that Chaucer could have said, but Chaucerian English would be woefully inadequate in the modern world. Grammatical differences are also obvious. The first and most important of these concerns recursion itself, the lack of subordinate clauses or embedding, which is very weak or even absent in the simpler languages, and instead we find strings of short phrases strung together paratactically with very simple SOV/SVO syntax and minimal use of pre/postpositions. In fact Progovac provides examples of "root small clauses" also lacking the "Tense Phrase" layer of the verb, and these can be used in complex languages as well as simpler ones. Examples in English speech are "Problem solved", "Case closed", "Point taken", or in Serbian "Stigla pošta", "arrived [past participle] mail"; "Pala karta", "Fell [past participle] card", "Card played". Progovac suggests that "some languages make predominant or sole use of small clause grammars" such as Riau Indonesian, Piraha, and Proto-Indo-European" (ibid., 88). Apart from these root small clauses with no finite verb form, in simpler languages there may be no recursion or embedding, and the interpretation is typically confined to the here-and-now (Progovac 2014: 86). We also find a lack of relative pronouns; the repetitive use of conjunctions; no passive voice; no conditionals; a weak tense and mood system; no case markers; very limited use of prepositions; no comparatives or superlatives; no numbers; little in the way of logical quantifiers (some, all, each, every); or little or nothing in the way of intensional verbs—assume, want, think, believe—that might require embedding.

I shall argue that these features of the simple languages are closely related to small homogeneous communities where strangers are relatively few, where there is low division of labour, where technology is of a simple subsistence type, and where there is no literacy or schooling. In other words, where utterances are *heavily context-dependent*. Literacy, on the other hand, is a crucial factor in the development of linguistic complexity, together with social size and cultural differentiation and heterogeneity. If, then we dismiss the belief in a language organ or module our only alternative is to propose a dialectical, constructive relationship between the properties of the human mind and the social relations between the individuals concerned. I therefore agree entirely that:

> ...*grammar is the product of history (the processes that shape how languages are passed from one generation to the next) and human psychology (the set of social and cognitive capacities that allow generations to learn a language in the first place). More important, this theory proposes that language recruits brain systems that may not have evolved specifically for that purpose and so is a different idea to Chomsky's single-gene mutation for recursion. (Ibbotson & Tomasello 2016: 74)*

In order to pursue this line of enquiry we must begin with the acquisition of language in ontogeny. It seems clear that a fundamental and unique characteristic of the human mind that is a necessary condition for language acquisition is what Tomasello has called "joint attention". Joint attentional skills emerge together at around nine to twelve months. Before this point infants typically interact either with objects or with people, dyadically, without coordination. But at this point:

> ...*a new set of behaviors begins to emerge that are not dyadic, like these early behaviours, but are triadic in the sense that they involve a co-ordination of their interactions with objects and people, resulting in a referential triangle of child, adult, and the object or event to which they share attention.... Most prototypically, it is at this age that infants for the first time begin to flexibly and reliably look where adults are looking (gaze following), to engage with them in relatively extended bouts of social interaction mediated by an object (joint engagement), to use adults as social reference points (social*

referencing), and to act on objects the way adults are acting on them (imitative learning). (Tomasello 2000: 62)

In particular, it is at this time that children start declaratively pointing to or holding up objects to gain the attention of adults not to themselves but to outside objects. "Declaratives are of special importance because they indicate especially clearly that the child does not just want some result to happen, but really desires to share attention with an adult" (ibid., 63).

On the other hand, by contrast:

Chimpanzee gestures are essentially imperative, designed to bring reward or advantage to the gesturer. That is, the chimp is requesting something, rather than making a statement. Studies of the use of signs by chimpanzees and bonobos in their interactions with humans have shown that 96-98 percent of their signs are imperative, with the remaining 2-4 percent serving no apparent function.... In marked contrast, human language includes declarative statements as well as imperative ones. We talk in order to share information, rather than merely request something for ourselves. (Corballis 2011: 163)

Chimpanzees are also very poor at auditory imitation and not much better at imitating what they see (Hauser, Chomsky & Fitch 2002: 1575). Tomasello has shown that it is the unique qualities of human social interaction that provide an essential basis for the creation of language as a collective representation. Human cultural learning is made possible:

...by a single very special form of social cognition, namely, the ability of individual organisms to understand con-specifics as beings like themselves *who have intentional and mental lives like their own. This understanding enables individuals to imagine themselves "in the mental shoes" of some other person, so that they can learn not just* from *the other but* through *the other. This understanding of*

others as intentional beings like the self is crucial in human cultural learning because cultural artifacts and social practices—exemplified prototypically by the use of tools and linguistic symbols—invariably point beyond themselves to other outside entities: tools point to the problems they are designed to solve and linguistic symbols point to the communicative situations they are designed to represent. Therefore, to socially learn the conventional use of a tool or a symbol, children must come to understand why, to what outside end the other person is using the tool or symbol, that is to say, they must come to understand the intentional significance of the tool use or symbolic practice—what it is "for", what "we", the users of the this tool or symbol, do with it. (Tomasello 2000: 5-6)

Again, "teaching is a form of altruism, founded on a motive to help, in which individuals donate information to others for their use" (Tomasello 2009: xiv), and humans actively teach each other things without regard to kinship. Even before speech develops, infants will try to provide information to adult strangers who need it by pointing, but apes do not understand this type of informative pointing at all. They do sometimes point at humans, but only to indicate that they want something for themselves; on the other hand, "Confronted with pointing, [human] infants appear to ask themselves 'why does *she* think that my attending to that cup will be helpful or relevant to *me*?'" (ibid., 18).

Infants also have an innate grasp of rules, in the sense of readily understanding that things *should* be done in a certain way, and try to enforce this. Children therefore legislate norms by themselves, regardless of parental instruction, even when not immediately involved in an activity, so that, observing a solitary game, they will condemn a puppet who is introduced and then disobeys the rules. The notion of the ideal way of how a game ought to be played follows directly from watching an adult, and children don't need to see the adult corrected. So rules are not just instrumental guides to the children's own effective action, but "are supra-individual entities that carry social force independently of such instrumental considerations" (ibid., 38).

Pattern-recognition, in which humans are specially adept, is also another crucial aspect of language acquisition, particularly during the sensori-motor stage of development. Evans (2014: 120) summarises these as:

The ability to relate similar objects and events, resulting in the formation of perceptual and conceptual categories for objects and events. Category formation aids recognition of events and objects.

The ability to form sensorimotor schemas based on recurrent perception of action. This is associated with the acquisition of basic sensorimotor skills, and the recognition of actions or events, such as crawling, walking, picking up an object, and so on.

The ability to perform distributional analysis on perceptual and behavioural sequences. This allows infants to identify and recognise recurrent combinations of elements in a sequence and thus identify and recognise sequences.

The ability to create analogies (recognition of similarity) between two or more wholes (including utterances, based on the functional similarity of some of the elements in the wholes.

We have, then, ample evidence for a number of innate dispositions in children that facilitate their acquisition of language: joint attention, social referencing, information sharing, imitative learning, and the grasp of rules, to which should be added skill in pattern recognition and sufficiency of short-term-memory. Children acquire a good, though not complete, mastery of grammar by around the age of 5 or so, which is well before they can fully grasp concrete operational thought, still less formal operations. This is presumably because, unlike the physical world about which they have to construct their own representations, language is not only presented to children ready-made, but is made by beings with the same minds as the children who are learning it.

The earliest language of our ancestors would presumably have resembled that of children in many respects, and Jackendoff and Wittenberg (2014: 68-72) sketch out a plausible model for the early stages of language, which like that of children would have begun as a one-word "grammar". But while this could not involve syntax it could be greatly enriched by "pragmatics"—real life content. In the case of infants' speech, "For instance, 'doggie' can be used to mean 'there's the doggie', 'where's the doggie', 'that looks like a doggie', 'I want the doggie', 'doggie pay attention to me', and so on" (ibid., 71) depending on what the situation is.

The next step is a two-word grammar, the number two being significant because this introduces a semantic relation between the words. "We speculate that this new semantic relation is the real source of complexity in two-word utterances" (ibid., 68n.3). The two word grammar then develops into a "concatenation grammar" consisting of strings of words of indeterminate length, but still without syntactic categories like nouns and verbs. Simple phrase grammars then follow, in which phrases are distinguished from words in the utterance: "[A]t this point in the hierarchy it starts to become useful to introduce parts of speech (or syntactic categories) to label words and phrases, yielding a part-of-speech simple phrase grammar. In such a grammar, different categories of phrases may specify different categories and orders for the words they contain" (ibid., 69). When it becomes possible to group phrases into higher order phrases, recursion finally becomes possible and syntactical structures develop.

But Jackendoff and Wittenberg point out the crucial role in this process of semantics and what they call "pragmatic enrichment" at the interface between utterance and meaning, which can be applied to much more complex utterances than one-word grammars. "They invoke only linear order and semantic distinctions such as object vs. action, argument vs. modifier, agent vs. patient, and topic vs. focus. They show how a fairly expressive language could be constituted without syntactic categories and even without phrase structure" (ibid., 77).

This is an appropriate point to review Hockett's claim, mentioned earlier, that "all languages have about equally complex jobs to do", which is the exact opposite of the truth. In our society language is employed in a vast diversity of ways through the medium of writing: literature, the natural and social sciences, technology, journalism, law, theology, and philosophy, for example, quite apart from all the occasions of its spoken forms both in the news media and face-to-face. On the other hand, in primitive societies there is, of course, no writing, and conversation is focused on the concrete and practical, so that all language is experienced in the context of daily life. In my experience of the Konso and Tauade uses of language, the telling of stories does not involve any apparent changes in syntax from that found in ordinary conversation. There are few strangers, and everyone shares the same general experience, with little specialisation of labour, apart from considerations of gender and age.

There are, in particular, no schools or formal instruction or lectures from adults; on the contrary, children learn practical tasks in the context of daily life by participating in the activities. Gradually the child is inducted into the full life of an adult. He is almost never told what to do in an explicit, verbal, or abstract manner. He is expected to watch, learning by imitation and repetition. Education is concrete and nonverbal, concerned with practical activity, not abstract generalization. There are never lectures on farming, house-building, or weaving. The child spends all his days watching until at some point he is told to join in the activity. If he makes a mistake, he is simply told to try again (Gay and Cole 1967: 16; see also Fortes 1938 for detailed confirmation of this).

The general principle at work here is that the richer the contextual information of utterances, the less load needs to be placed on syntactical structures to supply meaning:

Our idea is that the simpler grammars in our hierarchy put more responsibility for comprehension on pragmatics and discourse context.

*For instance, to understand a child's one-word utterance, one needs to
rely heavily on inferences about what the child might have in mind.
As the child's grammar acquires more grammatical devices, it provides
more resources for making complex thoughts explicit, reducing the
workload on the hearer. One could say that the syntactic complexity
of a maturing speaker is gradually easing the semantic and pragmatic
burden on the hearer. (Jackendoff and Wittenberg 2014: 66)*

6. Some examples of simple languages

To illustrate this extremely important point I shall give some examples
from non-literate cultures whose communication was exclusively oral,
so that meaning was heavily dependent on real-life contexts. The most
celebrated example of a society with a very limited grammar which
also lacks recursion is that of the Piraha of the Amazon, as described
by Daniel Everett, a professional linguist who originally went there as a
missionary. His work has been claimed as a fundamental challenge to
Chomsky and initiating a revolution in linguistics, but from what we
have seen of developments in linguistics in recent decades, the claims
of Universal Grammar, and especially about the central importance of
recursion have actually been obsolescent for some time.

The Piraha are a small population of a few hundred hunter-gatherers
with a very simple material culture, living in villages on the banks
of a tributary of the Amazon, who have been in contact with the
Portuguese for more than two hundred years, and with missionaries,
but who refuse to become acculturated. Everett describes the occasion
when he first realised that the Piraha have no recursion as follows:
"[O]ne day Kohoi was making a fishing arrow and needed a nail for
the tip. He spoke to his son, Paita: 'Hey Paita, bring back some
nails. Dan bought those very nails. They are the same'" (Everett
2008: 227). Apparently the Piraha language does not have relative
clauses that would allow them to say "Bring back the nails that Dan
bought" instead. But, despite this limitation in their language, the

Piraha can clearly *understand* the idea that has been expressed by the relative clause here; it is simply that they have to use a circumlocution to express it. The Piraha language also has a very limited grammar in other respects, which can be summarised as, besides no recursion or subordinate clauses:

> ...*no relative pronouns; only single modifiers; only one possessor; no co-ordinates such as "John and Bill came today"; no disjunctions e.g. "either Bob or Bill will come"; only one verb and one adjective in a sentence; no comparatives or superlatives; no counting; no distinction between singular and plural; no quantifiers—some, all, every, none; nouns have no prefixes or suffixes; no colour terms; no passive constructions; word order is not strict; no phatic communication (no greetings or farewells, "please" or "thank you" etc.).*

Everett maintains, quite rightly, that culture has a powerful influence on language, and claims that many features of Piraha culture and language can be explained by what he calls the Immediacy of Experience Principle (IEP). With regard to Piraha grammar he says:

> *Embedded sentences rarely, if ever, are used to make assertions. So the IEP predicts that the Piraha will lack embedded sentences because declarative utterances may contain only assertions. (234-5) It predicts that P will lack coordination because this also involves the general property of recursion. (236) The IEP's restriction against recursion also correctly predicts that P will lack disjunction, as in* Either Bob or Bill will come... *because it, like co-ordination, involves putting phrases inside of other phrases—recursion.... [T]he IEP helps to account for the other gaps in the language ... such as the absence of numbers and numerals, the absence of color words, the simplicity of the kinship system, and so on. (237)*

The IEP is also claimed to explain why the Piraha have no rituals or myths:

This principle states that formulaic language and actions (rituals) that involve reference to non-witnessed events are avoided. So a ritual where the principle character could not claim to have seen what he or she was enacting was prohibited.... [T]he idea behind the principle is that the Pirahas avoid formulaic encoding of values and instead transmit values and information via actions and words that are original in composition with the person acting or speaking [or witnesses or told by a witness]. So traditional oral literature and rituals have no place. (ibid., 84)

The IEP is also said to account for the very simple Piraha kinship system. The kinship terms do not extend beyond the lifetime of any given speaker in their scope and are thus in principle witnessable—[e.g., one's grandfather can be met, but not one's great-grandfather] (ibid.,133).

Here I must record my agreement with Sampson in his interview with Everett, when he says "I also wonder why it is important to you to derive diverse properties of Piraha from a single, simple abstract principle such as Immediacy of Experience. This feels like the kind of intellectual move that is attractive to the true believers in innate knowledge of language" (Sampson 2009b: 224). Everett's ethnography of the Piraha is thin by anthropological standards, but one can make out enough of their social organization and culture to conclude that there are problems with taking the Immediate Experience Principle as some distinctive feature of their culture. By this I mean that if we take into account the comparative literature on hunter-gatherers, and also the findings of cross-cultural developmental psychology the IEP turns out to be a familiar feature of hunter-gatherer culture, albeit developed to an extreme degree, but with which anthropologists are already familiar. Foragers are generally characterized by fluid group organization, individual freedom of movement and group membership, immediate and relatively easy access to resources, immediate consumption, simple division of labour, and relatively direct personal leverage over other individuals (Honigman 1968; Cohen 1985: 99-100). Morris (1991: 266-67) also refers to a normative stress on symmetric relations and egalitarianism, both between parents and children and between the sexes; second, a normative stress on self-sufficiency... third, a general looseness of social ties so that camps are 'shapeless, unstructured aggregations' of related kin, there being no corporate groups of any kind.

It has also been observed by various anthropologists (e.g., Gardner 1966, Morris 1976, 1991) that while the members of hunter-gatherer societies unsurprisingly have a great deal of practical knowledge of their environment, not only are their taxonomic systems limited in scope but they have a relative unconcern with systematisation (Morris 1976: 544). Gardner refers to this as memorate knowledge, that is, knowledge based on personal, concrete experience, and it has been noted as a characteristic of a wide range of hunter-gatherer societies, as well as some shifting cultivators. It extends to social relations as well as to the natural world, and Gardner for example says of the Paliyans, "Just as [they] have problems with natural taxonomy, they manifest difficulty providing models or rules to describe social practices such as residence" (Gardner 1966: 398). We can see that all these features apply quite well to the Piraha.

For example, it should be noted that the Piraha mode of classifying kin is about the simplest possible. All we have are a few categories basically referring to generation, and not even confined to actual kin: *baixi* = parent, grandparent, or someone to whom one wishes to express submission, e.g., a Brazilian, or a term of affection for the elderly. *xahaigi* = sibling, male or female, and it can also refer to any Piraha of the same generation. There is also *hoagi* = son, and *kai* = daughter (ibid., 86). It is not even certain that there are distinct terms for "mother" and "father", but Everett is not very clear on this. The lack of number terms is also a good example of this weak classification, but while the Piraha are an extreme case we noted earlier that many hunter-gatherer cultures and also some shifting cultivators may only have words for single, pair, and many. Again,

Everett remarks (ibid., 119) that Piraha lacks logical quantifiers like *all, each, every*, so that the word one might try to translate as "all" really only means something like "large amount", and so on. But, like so many other features of Piraha culture, this is a typical feature of primitive thought. For us, "some" and "all" are fundamental notions of logic and basic to propositions of inclusion which relate parts to wholes. So "all" denotes the totality of a set A, while "some" denotes "A − x" (where x is greater than 0). In primitive usage, however, we often find that while words are used that ethnographers translate as "all" and "some", "all" does not denote "all possible members of set A", but "all those in our experience" or simply "a lot" (see Hallpike 1979: 181-2). In so far as primitive thought is not usually concerned with working out the theoretically maximum number of items in a set, it will therefore tend to use "all" in the Piraha sense of "very many".

Everett strongly denies that the thought of the Piraha is primitive: "There is nothing in what I have written that should be interpreted as making the Pirahas or their language seem intellectually crude. Rather, what should be concluded is that their language fits their culture and their culture fits their needs and their environment" (in Sampson 2009b: 228). This, however, is an entirely circular type of argument: it is self-evident that the culture and organization of any society that has survived to be studied must be adequate to its "needs", or else all its members would be dead. The Piraha illustrate that it is possible for a society that is strikingly lacking in intellectual resources nevertheless to survive perfectly well. But we are also entitled to compare them with other societies and say that, for example, that a culture with no system of counting at all is less developed than a culture whose members can count up to a thousand. Again, it is particularly remarkable that the Piraha are said to have no myths or similar stories of any kind (ibid., 133) which may be unique in the ethnographic record. They even lack the idea of left and right (ibid., 215-16), which develops in children in modern society by 5 or 6 years of age and often earlier than that. The

Piraha also seem remarkably inarticulate, if the following story is any indication:

A man Xopisi had a wife Xaogioso who died alone in childbirth since no one would help her (we are not told who Xoii is):

> *"Xoii spoke. Xopisi is not here. Xoii then spoke. Xaogioso is dead. Well, he was called. I called Xoii. The only one. I thus spoke to Xoii. Xaogioso has died, Xaogioso. Xoii did not go to see her on the floating dock. Xagioso is really dead. Well, I am really fearful. Xoii then spoke. Xitaibigai did not tell about it. He said she did not tell. Xaogioso, do not die! I then spoke. Xaogioso has become dead. She is no longer here. Xoii did not go to see her on the floating dock." And so on, and so on. (ibid., 91-2)*

The reader may well find this as vague, rambling and unintelligible as I do, and I can certainly say that it has no resemblance at all in these respects to any text I was given during my fieldwork, where my informants both in Papua New Guinea and Ethiopia were quite capable of giving coherent accounts of events.

The Konso of Ethiopia with whom I lived from 1965-67 seemed to use no subordinate clauses in the texts they dictated to me, and certainly had no relative pronouns; so, for example, instead of saying "He is a man who tells good stories" they would say, like us, "He is a good story-teller". Nor did they use indirect speech; there was no disjunction such as "either Killano or Sagara will come"; no comparatives or superlatives; and limited use of adjectives and adverbs. They preferred to speak in sequences of short phrases which they could nevertheless use very effectively to convey meaning. For example, one night there was heavy rain, and the men ran out to their fields to make sure that the water was flowing properly in the irrigation channels. I went along with them to observe, and many of them were naked to prevent their cotton shorts getting uselessly wet, and my presence caused them a little embarrassment. Next morning one of them said to me 'Guiada xayti, halketa xanno', 'day yours night ours', which would have been meaningless if said out of context, but which was clear enough in these particular circumstances: "The day is public space where you can ask about whatever you like, but the night is our private space and we are not happy for you to intrude on it uninvited."

The following text is a good illustration of how they could tell a story with a minimum of syntactical complexity:

7. "The Bull that had a Calf"

I will first translate this into standard English, and then provide the original in the Konso language with a literal translation:

The Lion owned a bull, and the Monkey owned a cow. On one day the Lion would look after both animals, and the next day it was the Monkey's turn to do this, and so on. The Monkey's cow gave birth to a calf on the day when it was the Lion's turn to look after them. The Lion went and said, "My bull has had a calf." The Monkey said "My cow has had the calf. How can a bull give birth?" And the Lion says, "We will ask the elders of the animals if a bull can give birth." All the elders gathered except the Hare. They all went and asked him why he was not coming. The Hare replied "My madeda [a flat stone used in the removal of seeds from raw cotton] is broken, and I am stitching it together." "But how can a stone be stitched?" they all asked. "And how can a bull give birth?" the Hare replied. So the Monkey took his calf, and defeated the Lion.

Garma horma irqaba	Lion bull has
Keltayta okata irqaba	Monkey cow has
olini iseegini	together they take turns
guiada taka Garma	day one Lion
guiada taka Keltayta	day one Monkey
okata aKeltayta ixayte	cow of Monkey gave birth
guiada sede Garma okata idawe	day this Lion cow herded
Garma igalle ga geeni	Lion went and says

"hormayo ixaye"	"my bull gave birth"
Keltayta igeeni	Monkey says
"okatayo ixayte	"my cow gave birth
horma ata ixayni?"	bull how gives birth?"
Garma ga igeeni	Lion and says
"gimayta garaye ingassana	"elders among we will ask
ata horma ixaye"	how bull gave birth"
gimayta apinana pisanta ide	elders of animals all came
Kubalata bata indene	Hare only not came
nama pisa igeeni	person all say
"maana den ingin?"	"why coming is not?"
Kubalata igeeni	Hare says
"madeda imajamde	"madeda has been broken
an'ga hedini"	I and am stitching"
orra abila igeeni	people other say
"ata hedini dagatae?"	"how you stitch a stone for?"
Kubalata igeeni	Hare says
"horma ata ixayni?"	"bull how gives birth?"
semala ori Keltayta	so then Monkey
Inaya okata iteyete	(of) cow took
Garma ipudame	Lion defeated

This type of story falls into a familiar Konso genre of animal stories used to make some point about life, very like Aesop's Fables, so none of the listeners is going to query the idea of wild animals owning cattle or preparing cotton; it is normal for people to take turns herding stock, and elders' councils are a basic Konso institution, so in this familiar context they can use very simple syntactic structures to convey the story without any need for grammatical recursion. But in the broader sense of course there is *conceptual* recursion, since each sentence has a clear part to play in building up the story as a whole, the point of which is the symbolic relationship of the type A : B :: C : D, as in bull : giving birth :: stone : being stitched.

While the Tauade language of Papua New Guinea had no relative pronouns either, instead they could sometimes use the following type of recursive construction: "I already know the story that Maia told": '*Na Maia tapue tsinat ulo vari*': "I Maia-told-story already know". The standard word order is SOV, whereas in the embedded clause it becomes SVO. But this construction would seem to struggle with more complex embedded clauses: "I already know that you gave a small pig to Avui": "I you gave small pig to Avui already know", and I did not encounter it. Generally, however, they avoided recursion and used the same concatenation of short sentences as did Konso speakers. I collected very large numbers of stories and did not find that they included subordinate clauses. There was also very limited use of adjectives and adverbs, there were no comparatives or superlatives, and verb structure was simple. While in Papua New Guinea from 1970-72 I also gained some experience of Tok Pisin, or Neo-Melanesian as it was known in official circles.

Some linguists consider that a pidgin is not a real language at all, but since pidgins have duality of patterning and discrete infinity they display the basic defining characteristics of language, and it would therefore seem more logical to regard them as very simple languages. After several generations Tok Pisin has become a widely used language of native speakers, a creole, and in 1957 Fr Mihalic compiled a grammar and dictionary which gives us a good picture of the language as it was at that time.

The vocabulary has been mainly taken from English and German, while the syntax is English with considerable Melanesian influence. It has traditionally been spoken by non-literate natives and by Europeans in the practical situations of daily life such as the plantation and the dockside, which provide meaningful contexts that would often not be available in written texts. It is significant, however, that recursion, the allegedly most distinctive trait of language, is actually one of the least developed aspects of Neo-Melanesian:

Neo-Melanesian as spoken by the New Guinean is characterized by simplicity of clause and sentence structure. The native speaker prefers the simple sentence. When he does use a compound sentence it is mostly a juxtaposing of independent clauses rather than a combination of subordinate and independent clauses. (Mihalic 1957: 57)

Again, while there are simple personal pronouns, "There are no real relative pronouns in Neo-Melanesian. Instead, clauses are simply juxtaposed in two general patterns: with or without a connective" (10). "What in European grammar we refer to as possessive, relative, reflexive, intensive, or distributive pronouns require in Neo-Melanesian either a phrase or a longer circumlocution" (8). Prepositions are also very limited: "Actually there are only two pure prepositions in Neo-Melanesian, namely *long* and *bilong*" (44). *bilong* can denote possession, *haus bilong mi*, my house, but also purpose or function, *gutpela bilong kaikai*, "edible"; origin, *sospen bilong graun*, "an earthenware pot"; or a characteristic, *man bilong toktok*, "a talkative man". *long* denotes a less close relationship than *bilong* and can stand for in, on, at, to, from, with, by, about, because, for, and there are also no real equivalents to the definite and indefinite articles. Conjunctions are: *na* for "and" as well as "or"; *no* is "not" or "or"; *tasol* ("that's all") is "but", "however": *mi lukautim, tasol mi no painim*, "I searched but did not find". Quantifiers are: all, *olgera*; some, several, *sampela*; both, two, *tupela*; many, *planti*; none, *no gat sampela*; other, *arakain* ("other kind"); same, *wankain* ("one kind"), each, *wanpela wanpela*. (This is the same as the Konso expression for "each": *taka taka*, "one-one".) Nouns are basically singular, and there is no regular plural form, such as the English suffix *–s*. Pluralisation is either indefinite, *ol haus* ("houses"), or definite, *tripela boi* ("three boys"). Verbs, too, are very simple: "Verbs have no real tense forms in Neo-Melanesian. Time relation outside of the present is expressed with the help of adverbial modifiers. The future requires *baimbai* ["by-and-by"]; completed action, either *bin* or *pinis*, e.g., *mi lukim pinis*, or *mi bin lukim* ("I have seen, I saw")" (ibid., 29). "There is no special

paradigm or form to express incompleted action in Neo-Melanesian"
and speakers use locutions such as *bipo* [before] ("formerly"). Again,
"There is no real form for the passive voice in Neo-Melanesian", which
requires circumlocutions, nor does the verb have inflections for mood.
The imperative, therefore, is *yu go nau*, "go now"; *nogut yu go*, "Don't
go". "May", "might", "could", "should" are all *ken* [can], *yu no ken
kilim man*, "You may not kill a person". There is no conditional verb
form, since this would imply the use of subordinate clauses which,
as noted, are avoided in Tok Pisin. "If" clauses and the syntactical
complications they produce in the English verb are avoided quite easily:
"If you had been here yesterday, you would probably have seen him"
is "*Asde sapos yu stap hia, natink yu lukim em*": "Yesterday suppose [if]
you stop here, probably [I think] you see him" (34).

But since Mihalic wrote his dictionary and grammar Tok Pisin has
become considerably more complex especially through its association
with literacy in newspapers and the news media, and in politics, and increasingly in the school system, and not only has the lexicon expanded
but grammar has predictably become more complicated.

Riau Indonesian is not a pidgin but a colloquial Indonesian used
in informal every-day contexts by the population of the Riau region,
who number around five million native speakers (Gil 2009a,b). While
it has a large lexicon it is basically used for oral communication and its
grammar is of exceptional structural simplicity.

As summarised by Jackendoff and Wittenberg (2014: 80), syntactic
parts of speech are not distinguished, there are a small number of affixes
which are completely unselective in what they are attached to, there is
no inflectional morphology, arguments can be freely omitted, the only
evidence for constituent structure comes from prosodic phrasing, and
the effects expressed by syntactic subordination in English are achieved
by syntactic parataxis plus pragmatic enrichment. For example, conditionals are expressed paratactically, e.g., "You shoot a cop, you go to
jail", and word order is generally free. Gil gives as a typical example
the sentence: *ayam makan*, "chicken eat", which is extremely vague and

simply expresses the idea of "something to do with chicken and eating", but which could mean "the chicken is eating", "the chickens that were eaten", "something is eating the chicken", and so on, depending on the context (Gil 2009a: 23). Much of the structural simplicity may result from the processes of language contact between indigenous Malay and immigrant Minangkabau (Gil 2009b). Although many of its speakers are also familiar with Standard Indonesian which has a grammar of similar complexity to many European languages, nevertheless:

> *One important domain in which the standard language is typically preferred is that of writing. However, it is striking that although most Indonesians nowadays can read and write, Indonesia remains a functionally illiterate society: people prefer to communicate orally rather than in writing (Gil 2009b: 30), in all walks of life.*

As we shall see, writing is a key factor in grammatical complexity. Finally, we also find many aspects of this simplified grammar among the uneducated of our own society, although Pinker disputes this: "Linguists repeatedly run up against the myth that working-class people and the less educated members of the middle class speak a simpler or coarser language" (Pinker 2015: 26). But Bernstein provides copious evidence that this is not a myth at all, and that the speech of the uneducated working class tends to have the following characteristics:

> *Short grammatically simple sentences; a preference for the active voice instead of the passive; a simple verb structure that limits the expression of process; simple and repetitive use of conjunctions; short commands and questions; infrequent use of impersonal pronouns as subjects [e.g., "one"] reliance on implicit meanings and idiosyncratic phrases; repetitious dialogue reinforcing affective elements in relationships and discouraging analysis; conjunctions not used as important logical distributors of meaning and sequence; rigid and limited use of adjectives and adverbs which restricts the qualification of objects and modifications of process. (Bernstein 1971)*

This is a small sample of the evidence that it is perfectly possible to have simple, sometimes very simple languages that function as an effective means of communication in an oral culture, and that this is even possible in large-scale societies like our own where there are major differences in educational levels and cultural opportunities.

8. Social factors responsible for grammatical complexity

If grammatical simplicity is associated with relatively small-scale, context-rich societies where information does not need to be precise etc, what are the main factors that produce grammatical complexity? I shall argue that the primary factors that remove context from communication are not just social size and division of labour, and differentiation of life experience in general, but writing, which not only allows communication that is no longer face-to-face, as is necessarily the case with oral communication, but which also has properties of its own that favour grammatical complexity: "Written discourse develops more elaborate and fixed grammar than oral discourse does because to provide meaning it is more dependent simply upon linguistic structure, since it lacks the normal full existential contexts which surround oral discourse and help determine meaning in oral discourse somewhat independently of grammar (Ong 1982: 38). It also eases the burden on the short-term memory of the writer, so that he can constantly check on how he is constructing a long sentence.

In the case of written utterances, "Without precise knowledge of the audience or immediate, simultaneous feedback from the audience… the writer is obliged to use words and syntax more accurately, deliberately, and elaborately. In conversation, the participants function as an immediate, concrete environment for one another" (Fondacaro and Higgins 1985: 86).

Chafe points out that spoken utterances occur in a series of spurts, which he calls "idea units". These are essentially clauses "containing one verb phrase along with whatever noun phrases, prepositional phrases, adverbs, and so on are appropriate, and … is about seven words long and takes about two seconds to produce…. It is rewarding to hypothesize that an idea unit contains all the information a speaker can handle in a single focus of consciousness" (Chafe 1985: 106). That is, the idea unit approaches the capacity of short-term-memory. In longer spoken utterances, "idea units are typically strung together in a chain, with a relatively small amount of subordination. The complex arrangements of clauses characteristic of written language are rarely exploited. Speakers do not have the time or mental resources to compose them. Idea units may be independent … or they may be linked by co-ordinating conjunctions, by far the most common of which is *and*." (ibid., 111). Written language, on the other hand, not only has longer idea units, "but places them in various relations of dependence" (ibid., 112). Examples of these relations of dependence are a variety of subordinate clauses, prepositional phrases, indirect questions and quotations, nominalizations converting verbs into noun phrases, and participles converting verbs into attributive adjectives (ibid., 108-110).

Finite clause subordination is the prime example of a complex feature of language, and there is actually very good evidence that this has evolved in the course of history. Referring to Deutscher's *Syntactic Change in Akkadian* (2000) Geoffrey Sampson observes:

Akkadian is one of the earliest languages to have been reduced to writing, and Deutscher claims that if one looks at the earliest recorded stages of Akkadian one finds a complete absence of finite complement clauses. What's more, this is not just a matter of the surviving records happening not to include examples of recursive structures that did exist in speech; Deutscher shows that if we inspect the 2,000-year history of Akkadian, we see complement clauses gradually developing out of simpler, non-recursive structures which did exist in the early records. And Deutscher argues that this development was visibly a response to new communicative needs arising in Babylonian society. (Sampson 2009a: 11)

Karlsson rightly states that typical everyday spoken language tends to be very brief and simple, and:

Before the advent of writing in the third millennium BC, the major expository genre was oral narrative, which has been shown to be aggregative and paratactic rather than subordinating. Phrases are strung together into loosely conjoined shallow sequences (Lord 1960). This pattern of ancient additive structure is found across the world. As a case in point, Leino (1975) analysed a section of the Kalevala *(402 lines of verse, some 1,300 words) and found only three subordinate clauses, all "when"-clauses embedded at depth immediately below the main clause. For comparison, 1,300 words of current written Finnish would typically contain some sixty finite subordinate clauses.... (Karllson 2009: 195)*

While he agrees that some pre-literate languages do make limited use of finite subordinate clauses:

...there is ample evidence, for example from Semitic, Indo-European, and Finno-Ugric languages that the emergence of more elaborate grammaticalized patterns of finite clausal subordination is related to the advent of written language, especially to the conventionalization of various written registers. Proof of this development is provided for instance by Deutscher (2000) for Akkadian, by W. P. Lehmann (1974) for subordinate clauses in Vedic, by O'Neil (1976) for subordinate clauses in Old English, by M. Harris (1988) for concessive clauses in English and Romance, and by König and van der Auwera (1988) for subordinate clauses in Dutch and German. (ibid., 195-96)

Kalmar refers to studies showing lack of subordinate clauses in Australian languages, hunter-gatherers in Siberia, the Bushmen of South Africa, the Ojibway of North America, and Benveniste's claim that proto-Indo-European did not have relative clauses. (Kalmar 1985:

158-59) He also describes in some detail the emergence of subordinate clauses in Inuktitut in response to the use of writing and familiarity with English (ibid., 159-64).

So, to sum up, the linguist F. N. Akinnaso gives the following characteristics of *written* as distinct from spoken language:

1. Preferential usage of elaborate syntactic and semantic structures, especially nominal constructions (noun groups, noun phrases, nominalizations, relative clauses, etc.) and complex verb structures.

2. Preference for subordinate rather than co-ordinate constructions

3. Preferential usage of subject-predicate constructions instead of reference-proposition

4. Preferential usage of declaratives and subjunctives rather than imperatives, interrogatives, and exclamations

5. Preferential usage of passive rather than active verb voice

6. Preferential usage of definite articles rather than demonstrative modifiers and deictic terms

7. Higher frequency of certain grammatical features, e.g., gerunds, participles, attributive adjectives, modal and perfective auxiliaries, etc.

8. The need to produce complete information or idea units and make all assumptions explicit

9. Reliance on a more deliberate method of organizing ideas, using such expository concepts as "thesis", "topic sentence", and "supporting evidence" (1982: 104, quoted in Goody 1987: 263-64)

According to Karlsson, the maximum number of levels for initial clausal embedding is two, for Central clauses is three, and for Final clauses is five. These maxima were reached by Akkadian, which then influenced Greek, which in turn influenced Latin (Karlsson 2009: 201-202) which then influenced the European languages. These in turn have been extremely powerful models for non-European cultures, especially through colonisation and more recently the United nations, for the official languages of other governments throughout the world.

And then, once this new language had been invented, generative linguists would come along and point to it as yet further corroboration of the idea that human beings share innate cognitive machinery which imposes a common structure on all natural languages.... I believe essentially that process has been happening a lot with Third World languages in modern times. (Sampson 2009a: 17)

It might seem rather obvious to most of us that writing would have an important effect on grammatical complexity, but "Earlier linguists had resisted the idea of the distinctiveness of spoken and written languages. Despite his new insights into orality, or perhaps because of them, Saussure takes the view that writing simply re-presents spoken language in visible form ... as do Edward Sapir, C. Hockett and Leonard Bloomfield" (Ong 1982: 17). UG makes the whole question of writing and literacy irrelevant in principle, so it is not surprising that Pinker in *The Language Instinct* does not mention it at all, but it is significant that the topic is almost as generally ignored in most of the other works on linguistics that I have consulted.

With writing comes schooling, which has further potential for grammatical development if it goes beyond mere rote learning. Schooling and formal education that involve taking the pupils out of the context of their normal daily lives and their active participation and discussion with their teachers is of particular importance. It is closely involved with the ability to explain verbally one's reasons for making particular choices in test situations, and it also seems to develop the search for rules for the solution of problems, and the awareness of one's own mental operations. But we should also remember that medieval European universities conducted philosophical and theological debates in Latin, and that disputation was a fundamental basis of ancient philosophy in Greece, India, and China. One is not saying, therefore, that verbal discourse *cannot* engage a high level of syntactic complexity, only that it requires special circumstances, including people who are already literate, to do so. Bernstein found that there were marked differences in schooling between users of the "restricted" and the "elaborated code":

> [T]he group whom Bernstein found using this [restricted] code were messenger boys with no grammar school education. Their expression has a formula-like quality and strings thoughts together not in careful subordination but "like beads on a frame" (Bernstein 1974 p.134)— recognizably the formulaic and aggregative mode of oral culture. The elaborated code is one which is formed with the necessary aid of writing, and, for full elaboration, of print. The group Bernstein found using this code were from the six major public schools that provide the most intensive education in reading and writing in Britain. (Ong 1982: 83)

It is an axiom of UG that all native speakers have equal competence in their language, so:

> The fact that native speakers vary in grammatical competence has deep implications for linguistics and related disciplines.... I suggest that many linguists have an ideological objection to native speaker variations in grammatical competence, which they regard as socially dangerous, in that they can be used to justify social discrimination based on class and race. I also suggest that generative grammarians have a theoretical objection to individual differences. They are committed to the notion of an innate universal grammar, and individual differences are fundamentally incompatible with this notion. (Chipere 2009: 190-91)

So once a written literature has developed in the context of high civilization it has a number of important consequences for thinking and consequently for the use of language. Michael Barnes lists a more critical attitude to tradition because literacy allows the documentation of the past; a greater awareness of language as a tool of thought and the expression of ideas; the promotion of more complex systems of classification and their organization into coherent systems; and the greater privatization of thought and the objectification of personal experience (Barnes 2000: 82-3). Halverson refers in general to "the preservative potential of writing" and its cognitive consequences:

[T]he amount of available information can increase far beyond the carrying capacity of human memory, individual or collective; it means that each generation of thinkers can therefore build on the work of its forebears without starting all over again, thus making possible a much more rapid advancement of knowledge than is possible under oral conditions; it means that thought can be communicated more easily and accurately over space as well as time; that it can provide intellectual stimulation beyond the possibilities of isolated oral societies; that it can, in short, expand the mind and sharpen intelligence. These are the kinds of possibilities—only possibilities— opened up by writing, all of them probable and rather obvious. (1992: 315-16)

The complex societies in which the written word becomes normal therefore develop a whole range of cultural subjects that require increasingly complex forms of thought: administrative documents, legislation, legal disputes and arguments, technical manuals for a variety of tasks, and more abstract interests such as the theory of government and philosophy, the natural sciences, and of course literature.

More generally, in modern literate languages such as English, often read from the newspapers or in novels, it requires far more elaborate syntactical structures than are needed in primitive societies in order to provide enough context of time, place, and social circumstances to make statements comprehensible. And in our society most people we meet are strangers with very different life experiences, especially due to the enormous division of labour in advanced industrialized societies.

We can also expect the expression *of more abstract thought* to require greater precision of language than is necessary for the communication of concrete ideas. For example, "skid– crash– hospital" conveys a perfectly comprehensible sequence of concrete events with no syntactical assistance at all, because we can easily visualise the circumstances referred to. But when we are trying to convey abstract ideas we have to supply the necessary conceptual context as we go along, and this requires very precise syntactical tools to make each sentence comprehensible. Such sentences often become extremely long and complex in order to integrate a number of ideas into an intelligible whole. For example:

> *Thus in spite of the important respects in which Aristotle's use of opposites resembles, and indeed is influenced by, earlier notions, his physical doctrine of hot, cold, dry and wet may and should be distinguished both from the hypotheses of modern scientific method and also from the vague accounts common in pre-philosophical myths and early philosophical cosmologies: for if this doctrine cannot be said to give rise to predictions which can be tested experimentally, it is, on the other hand, far removed from the myth that derives all things from Sky and Earth or from symbolic classifications of phenomena which deal globally with the entire spectrum of reality.* (G. E. R. Lloyd Polarity and Analogy *1966, p.85)*

Finally, it should be noted in relation to the notion of a genetically based language instinct that writing involves different brain functions and areas from those of speech:

> *[D]ifferent brain areas are involved in hearing speech and reading it, and different comprehension centers in hearing words and reading them…. This finding refutes the conventional theory of comprehension, which argues that a single center in the brain understands*

words, and it doesn't really matter how (by what sense or medium)
information enters the brain, because it will be processed in the same
way and place.(Doidge 2008: 308)

Writing, however, and especially *literacy*, is a very recent historical
development, and the differences in brain functioning that it produces
scarcely seem consistent with the idea of a hard-wired cognitive organ
of language.

9. Conclusions

The purpose of this paper has been to assemble some evidence and
arguments that language does indeed become more complex in relation
to social and cultural complexity, especially as a result of writing
and literacy, and cannot therefore be an instinct, organ or module
as Universal Grammar maintains. But from the beginning we have
encountered not just reason and evidence but the dominating influence
of a number of ideologies. By "ideology" here I mean opinions that are
held with complete devotion by True Believers and a determination
to reject or evade what non-believers would consider to be important contrary evidence. Skinnerian Behaviourism, for example, had
immense academic influence and claimed that the whole idea of the
mind was an illusion and that language did not convey thoughts but
simply consisted of stimuli that changed the hearers' behaviour. On
the other hand Chomsky and his school firmly believe that the brain is
essentially like a machine, of which language is an inherited component
and whose operation is specified by the genome, and has essentially
nothing to do with culture or social relations.

Daniel Everett, in an interview with Geoffrey Sampson (2009b:
215) is obviously deeply committed to cultural relativism: "The Piraha's culturally constrained epistemology can only be evaluated in
terms of the results that it gives the Pirahas relative to their own values.
Since it serves them very well, there is no sense in the idea that it is
inferior." We might choose to avoid terms like "inferior" as vague and

tendentious, but it is entirely valid to compare Piraha culture with that of other societies, and in this more general scheme of things it appears to be unusually primitive, and the fact that the Piraha themselves appear quite happy has nothing to do with the matter. (Remarkably, in his book (2008: 272) Everett also says that he no longer believes in truth, a strange position for one who has spent a great deal of time and effort trying to prove that Universal Grammar is false, or who wishes his work to be taken seriously at all.)

We have also noted that linguistics has been significantly distorted not only by a dogmatic refusal for many years even to consider the subject of linguistic evolution, but by the obsession of secular liberal academics with intellectual equality, displayed in particular by linguists and cultural anthropologists. The Christian view is that all human beings have moral dignity because we are all children of God, a relationship which renders *intellectual* equality fairly irrelevant. (God, indeed, has generally been regarded as favouring the simple over the learned.) Secular liberals, however, dismiss the idea of God as superstition and believe that we are just another animal species in a Darwinian world, distinguished from other animals in the struggle for survival only by our intelligence. Nevertheless they still want to cling on to the traditional Western belief in the brotherhood of Man, and they can only do this by a fanatical conviction about human intellectual equality, despite all the evidence to the contrary. Liberal academics, especially during the Cold War, were also accustomed to look down on their colleagues in the Soviet Union, whom they saw as slaves to Marxist ideology. Yet at the same time, of their own free will and without the excuse of secret police, gulags, and firing-squads they eagerly enchained themselves in liberal political dogma about human intellectual equality that is just as devoid of evidence as Lysenko's dismissal of genetics as bourgeois science.

Notes

I should like to record my thanks to Professor John Colarusso, Professor Norman Doidge, and Dr Iain McGilchrist for their very helpful comments on this paper.

1. Indeed, the unfortunate Professor Everett, celebrated for claiming that the Piraha have no grammatical recursion, has been denounced as a racist for implying that they are therefore subhuman, and denied permission to return to them (Bartlett 2012: 5).

2. It is interesting that, since descriptive linguistics in America was fundamentally concerned with field studies of the languages of the Native Peoples, the doctrine of equal complexity was not questioned at that time. But "When relative complexity was previously a live issue in linguistics early in the twentieth century, syntax was not specially central to the discussions" (Sampson et al. 2009: 270) which were more concerned with comparative phonology.

3. I am obliged to Prof. Dr. Georg Oesterdiekhoff for drawing my attention to this in an unpublished paper he was kind enough to send me.

4. Rather similar "parameters" go back at least to the universals of Greenberg (1966).

5. Tomasello claims that "...the ontogenetic process that Piaget hypothesized as crucial for infants' understanding of objects in space— namely, the manual manipulation of objects—cannot be a crucial ingredient since infants understand objects in space before they have manipulated them manually.... This ruling out of one potential developmental process is a significant scientific discovery" (Tomasello 2001: 50). It is a pity that Tomasello had not read Lourenço & Machado 1996:144, which conclusively refutes the infant studies cited by Tomasello.

6. Professor Colarusso has pointed out (personal communication) that languages with small phonological inventories, such as Polynesian, must have long words and so would find it difficult to utilize

embeddings, whereas at the other extreme languages such as Ubykh, with 81 consonants, can pack more in and so put less strain on working memory and therefore open the door to embeddings. So it is possible that phonology can have developmental consequences, although these seem to arise only in extreme cases of simplicity or complexity.

Some afterthoughts

Some of the theories we have been examining can fairly be described as the products of reckless ignorance—those of Harari, Girard, and Byrne, in particular, as well as some of the Just-So stories in Chapter 1 about prehistoric clothes and fist-fights. And evolutionary psychologists and their obsession with freeloaders, for example, do not think they need to give much attention to what anthropologists have written about primitive society because they think they already have all the answers they need in Darwinian theory. Arens, however, can hardly be placed in this category, since he is a professional social anthropologist who has also done fieldwork in Tanzania and the Sudan. As such, he knows perfectly well that ethnographers have to rely on native informants for much of their data, which for various reasons they may not be able to observe for themselves. So his denial of the reality of cannibalism cannot be ascribed to ignorance at all, but is the result of a political agenda which has been trying for some years to deny the existence of primitive society as a colonialist myth.

Professor Edmund Leach, for example wrote that:

> *In my view there is no significant discontinuity in terms either of structure or form between "modern" and "primitive" societies. The social anthropologist can find what he is looking for in either…. [I]s it possible to formulate a useful stereotype of what this notional entity "a primitive society" or "a savage (wild) society" is like? The answer is: No! (Leach 1982: 14)*

Professor Adam Kuper a little later compared the idea of primitive society to phlogiston or the aether, saying:

The idea of primitive society is about something which does not and never has existed. One of my reasons for writing this book is to remove the constitution of primitive society from the agenda of anthropology and political theory once and for all. (This is unashamedly a story with a moral.) (Kuper 1988: 8)

Their assertions that there is no such thing as primitive society actually rested on no evidence at all, as I have demonstrated with considerable detail in an earlier paper (Hallpike 1992), but Leach and Kuper were not really motivated by a scholarly concern with evidence but, as Kuper more or less admits, by moral indignation. Leach in particular practically foams at the mouth with indignation: for him the new science of anthropology in the nineteenth and twentieth centuries:

...rested on the basic premise that all non-Europeans are stupid, childish, barbarous and servile by their very nature... The contemporary primitive peoples...were 'living fossils'; their savage customs were horrid survivals from antiquity which served to illustrate both the stupidity and the depravity of the beast-like behaviour of our primeval ancestors. (Leach 1982: 16-17)

Obviously, if one claims that primitive societies are "Small-scale, face-to-face, without writing, money, or the state, organized on the basis of kinship, age, and gender, and with subsistence economies", as I put it in the Preface, then modern industrial nation-states are the exact opposite, and we know that there has been an historical or evolutionary process by which societies of the first type have developed into those of the second. One of the major factors in this process has been conquest, and in recent centuries this has taken the form of colonialism. At the time this was generally seen as an extension of progressive government to under-developed peoples: Beatrice and Sidney Webb, for examples,

SOME AFTERTHOUGHTS   177

pillars of the socialist Fabian Society, were keen imperialists for this reason. The colonial powers amalgamated large numbers of tribes into nation states with centralized governments, political and administrative systems and legal codes, literacy and education (especially in Africa, Papua New Guinea and elsewhere), monetary economies, hospitals, roads and railways and telecommunications, and access to the major world languages. These changes could only have been imposed by force, and while colonialism is now routinely denounced by liberals as racist, they choose to ignore the obvious-if-inconvenient fact that without a period of colonialism the newly independent nations would never have come into existence and their peoples would have no place at all in the modern world. But with the demise of the colonial empires, and aided by the new obsession with equality and human rights, and by the postmodern hostility to the idea of science, political attitudes and academic fashion have gone into reverse.

The anthropologist J. F. Hamill, in his *Ethno-logic. The anthropology of human reasoning* (1990) has provided us with an illuminating insight into how a moral and political commitment to equality can develop into a general anthropological theory. In explaining how he wanted "to build peace and avoid destruction" (no doubt very laudable aims) he says that "Among anthropologists I found a more compelling view [than Catholicism]: that different ways of life were equal; that no god had endowed anybody with any special standing. I saw how cultural relativism would weaken the excuses to justify racism, imperialism, and colonialism" (1990: 1). But he realised that cultural relativism could not explain some obvious universals in human society and culture, such as the human family whose patterns fall within a narrow range of variability. The solution to this dilemma was provided for him by Chomsky's theory of grammar: "[T]he transformational-generative theory constrains variability while placing equal value on all observed variants: there are always some forms that language cannot take, but all languages are equally complex and equally good" (ibid., 1). Now, he continues, just as we all have an innate knowledge of language we must all have an innate knowledge of culture too; "People are equipped at birth, or before birth, with all the knowledge they need to acquire culture" (ibid., 11), and "the way cultures vary is similar to the way languages vary". So now he can easily conclude that:

> *All people are essentially equal in their ability to become cultured, and all people encounter approximately the same amount of information in the process of enculturation. Thus it is untenable to maintain that one culture is "higher" or more complex than another. In reality, there are no simple or primitive cultures; all cultures are equally complex and equally modern. (106)*

Setting aside the factual absurdity of this claim, it should be obvious that, even if we did have an innate knowledge of language, it cannot follow automatically that we are also born "with all the knowledge we need to acquire culture". That is a quite separate claim that has to be justified by at least the same amount of cross-cultural research into human culture as linguists have devoted to language. Actually, however, while all normal human beings have an equal ability to *acquire* culture, all the evidence from cross-cultural developmental psychology and anthropology in fact shows that all people do not encounter the same amount of information in the process of enculturation, and do not develop cognitively to the same extent, as I showed in *The Foundations of Primitive Thought* (1979).

But what is really fascinating here is the underlying but obvious assumption that a moral belief, in this case in equality, can become the basis for accepting the *truth* of cultural relativism, and then for accepting the further truth of Chomskian linguistics because this produces the desired conclusion that all cultures are, like all languages, essentially equal. The most effective way of protecting the sacred idol of equality, the Great Fetish, against the assault of facts is therefore to dispense with the idea of truth altogether and replace it by moral earnestness. So anyone who doubts that the syllogism is a universal mode of reasoning is a "colonialist", anyone who claims that there is such a thing as primitive thought is a "racist", and anyone who thinks that biology plays a significant part in human nature is a "fascist". Not surprisingly, then, Leach could say that "Social anthropologists should not see themselves as seekers after objective truth", but more like novelists. Welcome on board the Ship of Fools.

References

Akinnaso, F. N. 1982. "On the differences between spoken and written language", *Language and Speech*, 25, 97-125.

Anderson, S. R., & Lightfoot, D. W. 2000. "The human language faculty as an organ", *Annual Review of Physiology*, 62, 1-23.

Arens, W. 1979. *The Man-Eating Myth. Anthropology & Anthropophagy*. Oxford University Press.

Arens, W. 1997, "Man is off the menu", *Times Higher Education*, 1310, 16.

Arens, W. 2003. "Cannibalism reconsidered", *Anthropology Today*, 19(5), 18-19.

Balikci, A. 1970. *The Netsilik Eskimo*. New York: Natural History Press.

Baker, M. C. 2001. *The Atoms of Language. The mind's hidden rules of grammar*. Oxford University Press.

Barnes, M. 2000. *Stages of Thought. The co-evolution of religious thought and science*. Oxford University Press.

Barry, H., Child, I., & Bacon, M. K. 1959. "The relation of child training to subsistence economy", *American Anthropologist*, 61. 51-63.

Bartlett, T. 2012. "Angry words: will one scholar's discovery deep in the Amazon destroy the foundations of modern linguistics?", *The Chronicle Review*, 20 March.

Beaglehole, J. C. 1974. *The Life of Captain James Cook*. Stanford University Press.

Bergen, B. K. 2016. *What the F. What swearing reveals about our language, our brains, and ourselves*. Basic Books.

Berndt, R. M. & Berndt, C. H. 1964. The World of the First Australians. An introduction to the world of the Australian Aborigines. London: Angus & Robertson.

Bernstein, B. 1971. *Class, Codes and Control.* London: Routledge & Kegan Paul.

Bickerton, D. 2007. "Language evolution: a brief guide for linguists", *Lingua,* 117, 510-26.

Bickerton, D. 2009. "Recursion: core of complexity or artifact of analysis", in *Syntactic Complexity,* eds. Givon, T., & Shibatani, M. 533-544. John Benjamin Publishing Company.

Brown, P., & Tuzin, D. (eds.) 1983. *The Ethnography of Cannibalism.* Washington: The Society for Psychological Anthropology.

Byrne, E. 2017. *Swearing is Good for You. The amazing science of bad language.* London: Profile Books.

Carrier, D. & Morgan, M. H. 2014. "Protective buttressing of the hominin face", *Biological reviews,* June (online Early View).

Chafe, W. L. 1985. "Linguistic differences produced by differences between speaking and writing", in *Literacy, Language, and Learning. The nature and consequences of reading and writing,* eds. Olson et al., 105-23, Cambridge University Press.

Chipere, N. 2009. "Individual differences in processing complex grammatical structures", in Sampson et al. (eds) *Language Complexity as an Evolving Variable,* 178-91. Oxford University Press.

Chrisomalis, S. 2010. *Numerical Notation. A comparative history.* Cambridge University Press.

Chomsky, N. 1957. *Syntactic Structures.* The Hague: Mouton.

Chomsky, N. 1959. Review of B. F. Skinner Verbal Behavior in *Language,* 35, 26-58.

Chomsky, N. 1975. *Reflections on Language.* New York: Pantheon.

Chomsky, N. 1980a. *Rules and Representations.* Columbia University Press.

Chomsky, N. 1980b. "On cognitive structures and their development: a reply to Piaget", in *Language and Learning, The debate between*

Jean Piaget and Noam Chomsky. ed. M. Piattelli-Palmarini. 35-52. Harvard University Press.

Chomsky, N. 1995. *The Minimalist Programme.* MIT Press.

Chomsky, N. 2010. "Some simple evo-devo theses: how true might they be for language?", in R. Larson, V. Déprez, & H. Yamakido (eds.), *The Evolution of Human Language.* (54-62). Cambridge University Press.

Claessen, H. J. M., and Skalnik, P. 1978. *The Early State.* The Hague: Mouton.

Cohen, M. N. 1985. *Health and the Rise of Civilization.* Yale University Press.

Cook, J. 2013. *Ice Age Art, The arrival of the modern mind.* London: British Museum Press.

Corballis, M. C. 2011. *The Recursive Mind. The origins of human language, thought, and civilization.* Princeton University Press.

Cosmides, L., & Tooby, J. 1992. "The psychological foundations of culture", in *The Adapted Mind. Evolutionary psychology and the generation of culture.* eds. J. H. Barkow, L. Cosmides, & J. Tooby, 19-136. Oxford University Press.

Curtis, V. 2013. "Why manners matter", *New Scientist*, 2935, 28-9.

Denny, D. 1986. "Cultural ecology of mathematics: Ojibway and Inuit hunters", in M. P. Closs (ed.) *Native American Mathematics*, 129-80. University of Texas Press.

Diamond, J. 1997. *Guns, Germs and Steel.* London: Vintage.

Doidge, N. 2007. *The Brain that Changes Itself.* London: Penguin.

Dumont, L. 1970. *Homo Hierarchicus. The caste system and its implications.* London: Weidenfeld & Nicolson.

Dunbar, R. I. M. 2003. "The origin and subsequent evolution of language", in *Language Evolution*, eds. M. H. Christiansen & S. Kirby, 219-34. Oxford University Press.

Dunbar, R. I. M. 1996. *Grooming, Gossip and the Evolution of Language.* London: Faber & Faber.

Endicott, W. 1923. *Wrecked Among Cannibals in the Fijis.* Salem, Massachusetts: Marine Research Society.

Evans, V. 2014. *The Language Myth. Why language is not an instinct.* Cambridge University Press.

Everett, D. 2008. *Don't Sleep, There Are Snakes. Life and language in the Amazonian Jungle.* London: Profile Books.

Fitch, W. T. 2010. "Three meanings of 'recursion' ", in *The Evolution of Human Language. Biolinguistic perspectives,* (eds) R. K. Larson et al. 73-90. Cambridge University Press.

Fodor, J. 1983. *The Modularity of Mind.* MIT Press.

Fondacaro, R., & Higgins, E. T. 1985. "Cognitive consequences of communication mode: a social psychological perspective", in *Literacy, Language, and Learning. The nature and consequences of reading and writing.* (eds.) D. Olson, N. Torrance, & A. Hildyard. 73-104. Cambridge University Press.

Ford, C. S. & Beach, F. A. 1951. *Patterns of Sexual Behavior.* New York: Harper Torchbooks.

Forsyth, D. 1983. "The beginnings of Brazilian anthropology: Jesuits and Tupinamba cannibalism", *Journal of Anthropological Research,* 39(2), 147-78.

Forsyth, D. 1985. "Three cheers for Hans Staden: the case for Brazilian cannibalism", *Ethnohistory,* 32(1), 17-36.

Fortes, M. 1938. *Social and Psychological Aspects of Education in Taleland.* Oxford University Press.

Fromkin, V., Rodman, R., & Hyams, N. 2010. *An Introduction to Language.* 9th ed. Boston: Wadsworth.

Gardener, P. M. 1966. "Symmetric respect and memorate knowledge", *Southwestern Journal of Anthropology,* 22. 389-415.

Gay, J. & Cole, M. 1967. *The New Mathematics and an Old Culture.* New York: Holt, Rinehart & Winston.

Gil, D. 2009a. "How much grammar does it take to sail a boat?" in *Language Complexity as an Evolving Variable,* 19-33. Oxford University Press.

Gil, D. 2009b. "Riau Indonesian: what kind of a language is it?", in *Kongres Internasional Masyarakat Linguistik Indonesia (KIMLI) 2009*, Masyarakat Linguistik Indonesia and Universitas Negeri Malang, Malang, 29-61.

Girard, R. 1977. *Violence and the Sacred*. London: Bloomsbury.

Girard, R. 1987. *Things Hidden Since the Foundation of the World*. Stanford University Press.

Goody, J. 1987. *The Interface Between the Written and the Oral*. Cambridge University Press.

Gould, S. J., and Vrba, E. 1982. "Exaptation—a missing term in the science of form", *Palaeobiology*, 8(1), 4-15.

Greenberg, J. H. (ed.). 1966. *Universals of Language*. 2nd ed. MIT Press.

Haidt, J. 2012. *The Righteous Mind. Why good people are divided by politics and religion*. London: Allen Lane.

Hallpike, C. R. 1977 *Bloodshed and Vengeance in the Papuan Mountains. The generation of conflict in Tauade society*. Oxford: Clarendon Press.

Hallpike, C. R. 1984. "The relevance of the theory of inclusive fitness to human society".

Hallpike, C. R. 1992. "Is there a primitive society?", *Cambridge Anthropology*, 16, 29-44.

Hallpike, C. R. 2008a. *The Konso of Ethiopia. A study of the values of an East-Cushitic people*. Bloomington, Indiana: AuthorHouse.

Hallpike, C. R. 2008b. *How We Got Here. From bows and arrows to the space age*. Bloomington, Indiana: AuthorHouse.

Hallpike, C. R. 2011. "Some anthropological objections to evolutionary psychology", in *On Primitive Society, and other forbidden topics*, 214-55. Bloomington, Indiana: AuthorHouse.

Hallpike, C. R. 2016. *Ethical Thought in Increasingly Complex Societies. Social structure and moral development*. Lanham, Maryland: Lexington Books.

Halverson, J. 1992. "Goody and the implosion of the literacy thesis", *Man* (n.s.), 27, 301-17.

Hamill, J. F. 1990. *Ethno-Logic. The anthropology of human reasoning.* University of Illinois Press.

Hauser, M. D. 2008. *Moral Minds. How nature designed our universal sense of right and wrong.* London: Abacus.

Hauser, M. D., Chomsky, N., & Fitch, W. T. 2002. "The faculty of language: what is it, who has it, and how did it evolve". *Science* 298, 1569-1579.

Hockett, C. F. 1958. *A Course in Modern Linguistics.* New York: Macmillan.

Holmberg, A.1969. *Nomads of the Long Bow. The Siriono of Eastern Bolivia.* New York: Natural History Press.

Honigman, J. J. 1968. "Interpersonal relations in atomistic communities", *Human Organization*, 27, 220-29.

Howell, S. 1989. *Society and Cosmos. The Chewong of Peninsular Malaysia.* 2nd edn. Oxford: Clarendon Press.

Hubert, H. & Mauss, M. 1964. *Sacrifice. Its nature and function.* London: Cohen & West.

Ibbotson, P., & Tomasello, M. 2016. "Language in a new key", *Scientific American*, November, 71-75.

Jablonski, N. G. 2010. "The naked truth", *Scientific American*, 302(2), 42-49.

Jackendoff, R., & Wittenberg, E. 2014. "What you can say without syntax", in *Measuring Grammatical Complexity*, eds. Newmeyer & Preston, 65–82. Oxford University Press.

Jennings, W. 2004. "The debate over *kai tangata* (Maori cannibalism): new perspectives from the correspondence of the Marists", *Journal of the Polynesian Society*, 120(2), 129-47.

Kalmar, I. 1985. "Are there really no primitive languages?", in *Literacy, Language, and Learning. The nature and consequences of reading and writing*, eds. Olson et al., 148-66. Cambridge University Press.

Karlsson, F. 2009. "Origin and maintenance of clausal embedding complexity", in *Language Complexity as an Evolving Variable*, 192-202. Oxford University Press.

Kittler, R., Kayser, M., & Stoneking, M. 2003. "Molecular evolution of *Pediculus humanus* and the origin of clothing", *Current Biology*, 13, 1414-1417.

Koch, K-F. 1974. *War and Peace in Jalemo. The management of conflict in Highland New Guinea*. Harvard University Press.

Koehler, O. 1951. "The ability of birds to count", *Bulletin of Animal Behavior*, 9, 41-5.

Laland, K. N., & Brown, G. R. 2002. *Sense and Nonsense. Evolutionary perspectives on human behaviour*. Oxford University Press.

Lindenbaum, S. 2013. *Kuru Sorcery. Disease and Danger in the New Guinea Highlands*. 2nd Ed. Colorado: Paradigm Publishers.

Lindenbaum, S. 2015. "An annotated history of Kuru", *Medical Anthropology Theory*, 2(1), 95-126.

Liperski, P. P. 2013. "Kuru: a journey back in time from Papua New Guinea to the Neanderthals" extinction", *Pathogens*, 2(3), 472-505.

Lourenço, O., & Machado, A. 1996. "In defense of Piaget's theory: a reply to 10 common criticisms", *Psychological Review*, 103(1), 143-164.

Lyons, J. 1970. *Chomsky*. London: Fontana.

Lyons, J. 1977. *Semantics*. 2 vols. Cambridge University Press.

Mair, L. 1962. *Primitive Government*. London: Penguin.

Marshall, L. 1976. "Sharing, talking, and giving: relief of social tension among the !Kung", in *Kalahari Hunter-Gatherers*, eds. R. B. Lee & I. De Vore, 349-71. Harvard University Press.

Martin, J. 1827. *An Account of the Natives of the Tonga Islands*. 2 vols. 3rd ed. Edinburgh: Constable & Co.

Matsuzawa, T. 1985. "Use of numbers by a chimpanzee", *Nature*, 315, 57-9.

McGilchrist, I. 2012. *The Master and his Emissary. The divided brain and the making of the Western world*. Yale University Press.

Mechner, G., and Guerrekian, L. 1962. "Effects of deprivation upon counting and timing in rats", *Journal of the Experimental Analysis of Behavior*, 1, 109-21.

Mihalic, F. 1957. *Grammar and Dictionary of Neo-Melanesian.* Westmead NSW:Mission Press.

Momigliano, A. 1975. *Alien Wisdom. The limits of Hellenization.* Cambridge University Press.

Morris, B. 1976. "Whither the savage mind? Notes on the natural taxonomies of a hunting and gathering people", *Man* (n.s.) 11, 542-57.

Morris, B. 1991. *Western Conceptions of the Individual.* New York: Berg.

Murdock, G. P. et al. 1961. *Outline of Cultural Materials.* 4th ed. New Haven: Human Relations Area Files.

Needham, J. 1956. *Science and Civilisation in China.* Vol. 2. Cambridge University Press.

Newmeyer, F. J. 2003. "What can the field of linguistics tell us about the origins of language?", in *Language Evolution*, eds. M. H. Christiansen & S. Kirby, 58-76, Oxford University Press.

Newmeyer, F. J., & Preston, L. B. 2014. *Measuring Grammatical Complexity.* Oxford University Press.

Ong, W. 1982. *Orality and Literacy. The technologizing of the word.* London:Methuen.

Pagel, M., & Bodmer, W. 2003. "A naked ape would have fewer parasites", *Proceedings of the Royal Society of London*, B, (Suppl) 270, 117-119.

Parker, R. 1990. *Miasma. Pollution and purification in early Greek religion.* Oxford: Clarendon Press.

Pepperberg, I. M. 1987. "Evidence for conceptual quantitative abilities in the African Gray parrot: labelling of cardinal sets", *Ethology,* 75, 37-61.

Piaget, J. 1980. "The psychogenesis of knowledge and its epistemological significance", in *Language and Learning, The debate between Jean Piaget and Noam Chomsky.* ed. M. Piattelli-Palmarini, 23-34. Harvard University Press.

Pinker, S. 1997. *How the Mind Works.* London: Penguin.

Pinker, S. 2015. *The Language Instinct. How the mind creates language.* London: Penguin.

Progovac, L. 2014. "Degrees of complexity in syntax: a view from evolution", in *Measuring Grammatical Complexity.* eds. Newmayer & Preston, 83-102. Oxford University Press.

Prusiner S. B., Gajdusek D. C., Alpers M. P. 1982. "Kuru with incubation periods exceeding two decades", *Ann. Neurol.* 1.

Ryan, C., & Jetha, C. 2010. *Sex at Dawn: the prehistoric origins of modern sexuality.* New York: Harper Collins.

Sahlins, M. 1979. "Cannibalism: An Exchange", with W. Arens, *New York Review of Books*, March 22.

Sahlins, M. 1983. "Raw women, cooked men, and other 'Great Things' of the Fiji islands", in Brown & Tuzin (eds), *The Ethnography of Cannibalism*, 72-93, Washington: Society for Psychological Anthropology.

Sahlins, M. 2003. "Artificially maintained controversies. Global warming and Fijian cannibalism", *Anthropology Today*, 19)6), 3-5.

Sampson, G., Gil, D., & Trudgill (eds). 2009. *Language Complexity as an Evolving Variable.* Oxford University Press.

Sampson, G. 2009a. "A linguistic axiom challenged", in *Language Complexity as an Evolving Variable*, 1-18. Oxford University Press.

Sampson, G. 2009b. "An interview with Dan Everett", in Sampson et al *Language Complexity as an Evolving Variable*, 213-29. Oxford University Press.

Sexton, J. 2015. "A reductionist history of humankind", *The New Atlantis*, No. 47, 109-120.

Soffer, O., Adovasio, J. M., & Hyland, D. C. "The Venus figurines. Textiles, basketry, gender, and status in the Upper Palaeolithic", *Current Anthropology*, 41(4), 511-525.

Tomasello, M. 2001. *The Cultural Origins of Human Cognition.* Harvard University Press.

Tomasello, M. 2009. *Why We Co-Operate.* MIT Press.

Tooby, J., and Cosmides, L. 1992. "The psychological foundations of culture." in (eds.) J. Barkow, L. Cosmides, and J. Tooby, *The Adapted Mind. Evolutionary psychology and the generation of culture*, 19-136. Oxford University Press.

Townsley, J. 2003. "René Girard's theory of violence, religion, and the scapegoat", www.jeramyt.org

Trigger, B. 2003. *Understanding Ancient Civilizations.* Cambridge University Press.

Uttal, W. R. 2001. *The New Phrenology. The limits of localizing cognitive processes in the brain.* MIT Press.

Vasey, P. L., & Vanderlaan, D. P. 2010. "An adaptive cognitive dissociation between willingness to help kin and nonkin in Samoan *fa'afafine*", *Psychological Science*, 21(2), 292-7.

Wade, N. 2007. *Before the Dawn. Recovering the lost history of our ancestors.* London: Duckworth.

Wagner, R. 1967. *The Curse of Souw.* Chicago University Press.

Wallace, A. R. 1871. "The limits of Natural Selection as applied to Man", Chapter X in his *Contributions to the Theory of Natural Selection*, 2nd ed. 332-71. London: Macmillan.

Whitehead, N. L. 1984. "Carib cannibalism: the historical evidence", *Journal de la Société des Américanistes*, 70, 69-87.

Whiting, J. W. M. 1968. Discussion in *Man the Hunter*, eds. R. B. Lee & I. De Vore, 336-38, Chicago: Aldine.

Wilson, E. O. 1978. *On Human Nature.* Harvard University Press.

Wilson, E. O. 2004. *On Human Nature.* 2nd ed. Harvard University Press.

Wober, M. 1974. "Towards an understanding of the Kiganda concept of intelligence", in (eds.) J. W. Berry & P. R. Dasen *Culture and Cognition: readings in cross-cultural psychology*, 261-80. London: Methuen.

Woodburn, J. 1968. Discussion in *Man the Hunter*, eds. R. B. Lee & I. De Vore, 91. Chicago: Aldine.

Woodruff, G., and Premack, D. 1981. "Primitive mathematical concepts in the chimpanzee: proportionality and numerosity", *Nature*,
293, 568-70.

About the Author

C. R. Hallpike is an English and Canadian anthropologist whose work covers a period of fifty years, and is unusually wide-ranging and diverse. Apart from extensive field work in Ethiopia and Papua New Guinea, he has made distinctive contributions to some of the most fundamental problems in the subject: cultural relativism, social evolution, primitive thought, the nature of religion, warfare, moral development, and even the origins of modern science.

CASTALIA HOUSE

CPSIA information can be obtained
at www.ICGtesting.com
Printed in the USA
FSHW012143050621
81995FS